For Norma Jean –
Thanks for being a fan
Rosemary Coplin-Dahlberg
"Rosie"
3-2016

Gravel and Grit
Childhood Memories of Life on a Kansas Farm

Rosemary Coplin Dahlberg

WESTBOW PRESS
A DIVISION OF THOMAS NELSON
& ZONDERVAN

Copyright © 2016 Rosemary Coplin Dahlberg.

All rights reserved. No part of this book may be used or reproduced by any means, graphic, electronic, or mechanical, including photocopying, recording, taping or by any information storage retrieval system without the written permission of the author except in the case of brief quotations embodied in critical articles and reviews.

WestBow Press books may be ordered through booksellers or by contacting:

WestBow Press
A Division of Thomas Nelson & Zondervan
1663 Liberty Drive
Bloomington, IN 47403
www.westbowpress.com
1 (866) 928-1240

Because of the dynamic nature of the Internet, any web addresses or links contained in this book may have changed since publication and may no longer be valid. The views expressed in this work are solely those of the author and do not necessarily reflect the views of the publisher, and the publisher hereby disclaims any responsibility for them.

Any people depicted in stock imagery provided by Thinkstock are models, and such images are being used for illustrative purposes only. Certain stock imagery © Thinkstock.

ISBN: 978-1-5127-2207-9 (sc)
ISBN: 978-1-5127-2206-2 (e)

Print information available on the last page.

WestBow Press rev. date: 12/28/2015

Thank you, Fred.
Without your encouragement, these memories would never be in print.

This is a collection of memories of my childhood. When I told these stories to my children, my eldest child, Mark, would say, "Oh, no! More museum pieces!" Because of that remark, I discontinued to recount my childhood events. My memories, however, never left me. It occurred to me that my three grandsons, who live in a city two hours away from me, had never heard of my life on the farm. Times have changed and things that are taken for granted now, were new and exciting 70 years ago (REA and indoor plumbing for example). My dear husband, Fred, who is an historian, urged me to write these memories down in a journal of past times.

I dedicate this writing to Mark and his wife, Norma, (Yes, more museum pieces!); my grandsons, Bryan, Steven, and Keith; my dear sister, Dorothy, who shared some of these times with me; and to Fred, who believes that he knows me better now that he has read my stories. I present these true accounts in memory of wonderful family members, friends, and pets that have completed their life's journeys and have made mine so enriched.

Forgive me if time lines don't historically match, or my events seem to be a little embellished -- but it was my life and it was how I remembered it. The following accounts show the reader my early roots and the blessings that I received from my wonderful Daddy and Momma on a typical Kansas farm in the 1930's and 40's. I labeled my experiences as "gravel and grit" because of the gravel roads, the dust, and the grit that made all of us Kansans a really hardy bunch.

Rosemary

The Hockenberry House

Everyone can recall their childhood home, especially if they lived there for several years. I can vividly remember the big two-story country house where I spent the first five years of my life. It was located in Washington County Kansas, five miles from the city of Washington. The city was small (about 1700); but it bustled with activity because it was the county seat.

The house was near an intersection of two gravel roads. This farm was owned by Ada Hockenberry, a widow who lived in Topeka. Daddy wanted to buy this property because he owned 80 acres of land that adjoined Ada's farm; however, she never wanted to sell. Therefore, Daddy rented her farm when he married Momma on February 28, 1935. Momma was a widow with two children -- Roy was 12 and Dorothy was 10. I was to come along on April Fool's Day, 1937.

The old house was a gray color -- not from paint, but from the lack of it. The boards had a weathered look about them and in some sheltered areas, the remainder of white paint could be detected. It must have been pretty in its younger days. Daddy and Momma didn't care about the outward appearance. It was the inside that was important to them and they cleaned and painted to make the rooms cozy and comfortable. The rooms were big and the ceilings were high. It gave us lots of room to grow.

The house didn't have a very big yard as it was near the gravel road that curved to the south. Our mailbox was located on the corner and we made a daily trek to eagerly pick up **The Topeka Daily Capital** and any letters or cards that occasionally came to us. A porch was on the front of the house; but no one ever came to that entrance. Perhaps strangers were hesitant to use the front because our black dog, Godlip, liked to lounge out there and keep an eye on cars and tractors; which he'd chase at every chance he got. Our side porch that led into the kitchen was the one everyone used. Daddy placed large planks of lumber to form a "sidewalk" so that mud and dirt wouldn't be tracked into the house.

It was on this porch that I delighted in hammering in tacks into the north wall. I'd wear my favorite coveralls -- gray with a pinstripe of red -- and a loop on the right side where I hung my hammer. Daddy asked Mrs. Hockenberry if it was all right for me to hammer tacks into the wooden wall. "Of course it is. It's an old porch any way. Maybe she can repair it, or perhaps her hammering on it will make it collapse!" Her jovial reply made me glad and I'm sure Momma was happy about the arrangement because it kept me busy for hours. Whenever Momma heard the "tap, tap, tap", she knew where I was and what I was doing. When there was silence, she'd call out, "Rosemary, what are you up to?" Once she heard a "tap"" on something that sounded like metal. Looking out the kitchen door, she spied me playing "auto mechanic" on the chrome bumper of the car. Somehow I had found a large spike and was using that instead of tiny tacks. Needless to say, that pretend occupation came to an abrupt halt. I was instructed to keep the hammer and tacks on the side porch and nowhere else. Also, the long spike had to be put back in Daddy's workshop.

In the kitchen was a light green Majestic cooking stove that used wood for its source of heat. Momma usually had a tea kettle simmering on the back of the cooking surface to keep humidity in the house in the wintertime. There was a wash-stand with a basin and pitcher for washing before meals. Water had to be carried in by the bucketful from the pump outside under the big Morse-Fairbanks steel windmill.

There was a roller towel on the back of the kitchen door for hand drying. I remember that roller towel! It was on Thanksgiving Day and Momma was preparing food to be taken to the Ash Creek School for our community dinner. I was bored and it was too cold to play on the porch or outside. I enjoyed the warmth of the kitchen and the wonderful aroma of pumpkin pies baking. With nothing better to do, I sat in the sling formed by the roller towel. Momma warned me not to sit in the towel because it would break the fastener at the top of the door. "Rosemary, get out of the towel!" Momma ordered. Being a contrary little imp, I remained in the towel, swinging back and forth. On the third warning, Momma wiped her floured hands and grabbed me at the upper arm to get me out of the towel. Then she gave me one big slap on the butt and told me to sit in the corner of the kitchen until we were ready to get dressed for the dinner.

Of course I made a big deal of it with tears streaming down my cheeks and gasping sobs coming from my slobbery mouth. Mother went on about her work cleaning the pastry board and checking on the pies in the oven. She didn't give me an audience, so I quieted down. When we went to the community dinner, Mr. Higgins, the Community Club leader, asked all of us to tell of what we were thankful. When it came to me, I stood up and in a pouty fashion said, "I don't have anything to be thankful for because I got a spanking this morning." Everyone giggled at this bratty four year old -- except Momma, who lovingly looked at me and smiled. In her eyes and in her smile I read her thoughts: "You deserved it!"

This simple farm house, without indoor plumbing and electricity, was the setting where we enjoyed a good family life. I passed by this old house in the summer of 2008. It stands today more weathered than ever, holding past memories for me. I didn't ask the current occupants if I could enter; I knew things would be different and I wanted to preserve the images of my childhood in my mind. Somehow seeing other people there would tarnish my memories. It was there in the Hockenberry House where my roots were formed and where my memories began. Let me share them with you.

"Tap, tap, tap. Oops! Don't hammer on the car!

Roy, Dorothy, and Me!

My arrival into this family was probably a blessing as well as a surprise. In the late
1930's it was somewhat uncommon for a bachelor, like my Daddy, to marry a widow

with two pre-teen children. Today in the year 2009, blended families are almost the norm. My birth was a blessing to my mother, father, and his parents; and I was probably a big surprise to my brother and sister. No matter what my status, growing up with an older brother and sister was so much fun. I was never in on any sibling rivalry because I was never in a position to beg or barter favor from either of them. Being the baby in the family entitled me to privileges that I really didn't deserve, but got anyway! I was a spoiled little girl -- how could I not be when I was the only child of Carl Dague, the only grandchild of George and Mary Dague, and the only baby in the house? Plus, I was cute!

I don't actually remember the fact that as a toddler, I loved green beans; but I was told that whenever Dorothy would mention the words "green beans, green beans", I would scrunch my nose, laugh, and wiggle around in my high-chair. Dorothy's girl friends would wonder why I liked that phrase and that vegetable. I have no answer for that; but I think that it was due to the attention that I got from my sister. She was very good to me. And, by the way, I still like green beans -- only I don't laugh about them now.

I was also told that I loved to get into things -- most three-year-olds do. When groceries were being put away after a shopping trip, I was usually given something to keep me busy and out of the way. One Saturday afternoon I was given a half-gallon tin can full of Karo Dark Syrup. It was newly purchased and therefore had never been opened. To open such a can took a great deal of energy and patience, plus a screw driver or paint can lid prier. I lugged the can around as best as a three year old could. The adjoining living room with its new area carpet looked inviting; so I went in there and plopped the can down, sat on it, and rolled around with it. This was really fun! As Momma and Dorothy put away the groceries, I was busy playing and pounding on the can. Then something happened -- the can lid popped out of the channel and a stream of thick brown syrup flowed out onto the new carpet. When Momma and Dorothy saw this, they couldn't believe their eyes. How could Rosemary have opened the can? Of course the play adventure was over. I was whisked out of the sticky, yet yummy mess; while Daddy and Momma cleaned the carpet and Dorothy cleaned me. The spot remained throughout the years and it was always brought to my attention whenever we moved the furniture at spring and fall cleaning. You see, the carpet was moved around so that the stain could be hidden by the davenport; but I was always reminded of the fact that the Karo Syrup and I were responsible for it.

Thank goodness our rooms were large with high ceilings. Our living room housed a big forest green wood and coal stove. It stood in a corner with a black stove pipe going up into the ceiling. A large davenport, a radio console, and a big oak library table with straight-back chairs alongside, plus a couple of rocking chairs filled the room. It was in this crowded setting that Roy and I played a game of "Wolf". He was the wolf and I was "Little Red Riding Hood. He'd tousle his dark brown hair and growl. Then the chase would be on! Round and round the stove we'd go; then stopping and dodging to see which way the other would go. It was so much fun. As I would go round and round, I'd get dizzy and silly. I'd laugh and tease Roy. One time my dizziness caused me to run smack-dab into the sharp corner of the library table. This accident caused a big gash in my forehead along the hairline. (I can feel the scar to this day.) I bled like a stuck pig and I can remember crying with the pain and at the sight of all the blood. This little event also caused the neatly lined books on the table to tumble, and the fragile mantles on the Coleman gas light to fall to a pile of gray ash. "All right, you two. Settle down", Momma commanded and she tended to my injury and ordered Roy to set the books upright. Daddy had to attach new mantles to the light. It was good that on another table out of the race-way, we had a coal oil lamp that used a wick for a flame; or we would have been in total darkness. Mantles were rather expensive, perhaps 25 to 30 cents a piece, so I was advised to never bump into the table again.

Roy also liked to play barbershop with me. He'd pretend to come in out of the wind and tell me that he needed a shave and a haircut. I'd take the tinfoil wrappers from Wrigley's spearmint gum and use the saw-toothed edges to give him a "really close shave." Then I'd take his comb and part his hair into funny styles. Sometimes he'd have a part on the right, then the left, then the middle, and then no part at all with his hair combed either forward or to the back. With each new style, he's make a funny face and that would make us all laugh. We'd play this over and over. I imagine his scalp would have been really sore; but he never mentioned it to me.

Roy had a little green Model A Ford with a rumble seat. I really liked to sit back there. Momma always worried and she'd caution Roy about not driving with me in the back. I'd beg and plead and finally Roy would give in and drive slowly around the tall windmill and down the lane to the barn. I felt very big to be sitting back there,--kinda like being the Queen of England, only on a much smaller scale. I often found interesting things back there -- a frozen bottle of 7-Up, a "church key" can opener, comic books, and coins. I got to keep the comics; but Roy wanted his money.

Dorothy was a lot of fun too. She was the best candy maker and I always wanted to "lick the pan" when the fudge was poured out on the buttered plate to cool. (To this day, I use the recipe that she used). Dorothy also taught me to put my straight brown hair up in pin curls. My little fingers couldn't manage too well, so my style never turned out as nice as hers. She also introduced me to nail polish. She was skilled in painting her nails a crimson color, leaving the half-moons of the nail near the cuticle bare. This manicure procedure was much too complicated for me. My stubby little nails didn't look good with the bright red polish; after all, I was lucky to get my hands clean after playing in the mud. I certainly didn't need to fuss with a manicure and polish.

Another fun time with Dorothy was to go down to the cellar to get a can of "guess what" for supper. The grocery store, owned by Paul and Cornelia Butler, had a fire and the smoke-damaged goods were sold without labels. In the 1940's people were looking for bargains, so two cans of food for a nickel was a good deal. The only problem was, we didn't know what the cans contained. That's why we called them "guess what". Dorothy and I would try to guess the contents of each can. Momma would allow us to pick two items. We would shake the cans and try to decide if they were peaches, pears, spinach, or God forbid, sauerkraut. Sometimes our suppers were a little strange. If we selected beets and hominy, that would cause some disgruntlement at the table; but we had to eat what we had chosen. As the weeks wore on, we got pretty good at guessing. When the cases of fire-sale cans were completely used, it was a little sad for the game to come to a halt.

When I started school, my friends wondered why my last name and my brother and sister's last names weren't the same. I had to explain that their daddy was Davenport and mine was Dague. "Oh, so they're only your half-brother and half-sister," my friends would say. I would immediately set them straight. They weren't "half" anything. They were my **brother and sister.** It never bothered me that our last names weren't the same.

However, I did think it strange that their last name Davenport was like the piece of furniture that we had in the living room. Did their daddy invent that? It seemed like a sensible idea to me. Today that piece of furniture would be referred to as a hide-a-bed.

Roy and Dorothy liked to teach me the names of their classmates. Some of the family names were pretty difficult to pronounce; but I learned them and I was always proud to "name the seniors" for Roy's class of 1940 and Dorothy's class of 1942. I'd get a step-stool and read the names from the framed class photos on the wall. Now realize, I couldn't read at that age; but I recognized the pictures and shouted out the names with glee. I can still recall a few of the seniors: Ival Brabec, Ray Fortner, Eddie Wohglemuth, Duane Wohglemuth, Ruby Roop, Don Van Amburg, Thelma Tegethoff, and Opal Rogers. That's pretty good to remember after all these years.

What a lucky little girl I was to have Roy and Dorothy as my brother and sister. All through my life, I was close to them. Although the age differences, along with the miles might have separated us; when Roy moved to Florida, and Dorothy to Wichita, Kansas, a cord of love connected us. I was truly blessed to have them in my life -- my childhood and my adult life were richer because of them. Roy passed away in 2003. Dorothy resides in Wichita and every Sunday I call her and give her my love.

Rock School House
Roy, Grandpa, Daddy, Dorothy, and Grandma
(Taken by Momma before I was born.)

Caption: Momma and me

Daddy and me

Spilt Milk

Momma was an excellent cook. With her tasty meals, one would assume that I was a "chunky" kid. That was not so. My skinny arms and legs led one elderly neighbor lady to remark to Momma, "You'll never raise that child, Clara. She needs more meat on her bones." What a thing to say when I was standing right in front of her. How would she have liked it if I had said that she was a wrinkled old hag with a dowager's hump?

My sister, Dorothy, was a good eater and consequently she did have meat on her bones. One time Daddy and Roy teased her after she had cleaned her plate and aked for "seconds". They called her "Greedy Gut" -- which Momma stopped in an instant. "There will be no talk like that around this table. You can call the piggies that, but not Dorothy." Because of her good diet, Dorothy had a peaches and cream complexion and pretty white teeth. She was a lovely girl and an envy to all her friends who suffered from the break-outs of acne.

My finicky palate only liked a few things -- anything chocolate, green beans, and Pepsi Cola. That diet didn't promote strong teeth or bones; something that I regretted in my later life. I can't fault Momma because she tried to get me to eat. She also loaded milk with Bosco or Ovaltine in order to tempt me to drink it.

My dislike for milk probably came when Roy and I were playing "Run, Wolf, Run" around the house. We weren't supposed to do that; but I teased and taunted him, and he chased me around the rooms right into the porch area where the milk separator was located. It was a stainless steel contraption that separated the cream from the milk. It was used every morning after the cows had been milked. Chilled milk from the milking on the night before would be added. When the milk and cream were separated, they would be taken down to the cellar to be put in the ice-box where a 50 pound block of ice was always placed.

The separating machine was wound by hand and when the process was almost finished, the machine would wind down on its own. The separating process was almost completed and Momma had gone to the kitchen cabinet for milk jugs. As I turned the corner, a large five-gallon pail of frothy milk was in my pathway. I tripped on a throw-rug and Splash! I landed headfirst into the white liquid, upsetting the pail and creating a huge mess. My gray cover-alls were soaked and the floor became slippery. Momma came running when she heard the commotion. "What's going on? Oh, my, look at the mess that the two of you have created." She shook her head in disgust and put her hands on her hips. She always did that when she was really mad. "How many times do I have to tell the two of you not to run around inside the house? I am really upset about all of this. Five gallons of milk have been lost. The two of you will have to clean it up all by yourselves. Then you'll have to change clothes, take baths, and you, Rosemary, will have to have a shampoo. Now get to work, both of you!" Momma was not only upset about the mess, and the loss of good milk; it was a busy wash day ahead for her. She didn't need this.

With that scolding and the litany of orders, Roy and I set about our work. We had to get old towels and rags to sop up the milk. Roy went to the well and pumped buckets of water for the cleaning. We used "Spic and Span" cleanser to cut the fat residue that the milk left behind. The warm morning sun made the milk take on a sour smell. That's probably why I have never liked milk and I can recall the smell of sour milk even as I write this. Roy did most of the heavy work; after all, he was older. I was only four; but he didn't let me get away with shrugging my share.

After an hour, the mess had been washed away. Then Roy had to put water on the wood stove to heat for our baths. He also brought in the round metal wash tub that we used for bathing. Since I was the dirtiest, I went first. As I swirled around in the water, washing every part of my body from stem to stern, I was really mad at myself for teasing Roy into that chasing game. Poor Roy had to do some heavy lifting getting the water and tub ready and it was really all my fault -- but then, he was older and he should have known better than to chase me indoors. I was trying to place the blame on Roy; but deep inside I knew that I had started it. I was to blame.

I dried myself and tousled my hair. "Momma, can I put on some of your talc?" I loved the scent of "Moonlight and Roses". It would dust away any hint of sour milk. Momma agreed and I began to feel better. "Momma, I'm sorry about the mess." I owed her an apology and I became her little helper for the rest of the day.

Luckily, it was wash day, so our milk soaked clothes would be cleaned and hung out to dry on the line. I suppose the soaked towels and clothes would have stayed in the hamper until the regular wash day. Remember, this was before electricity came to the farm; so bringing in the Speed Queen wringer washer, two tubs, and water from the well was not an easy chore. The washing machine was operated by a gas motor, so an exhaust pipe had to run from the motor to the outside. I was told many times to "Watch out for the hot pipe" and many times I'd forget and not clear it as I tried to jump over it. There are many burn scars on my shins documenting the miscalculations of my jumps.

Momma liked to use Oxydol or Duz soaps. We always started with the white clothes, followed by the colored ones, and ending with the grungy bib-overalls. I wondered if the overalls ever got really clean after churning in all the dirty water preceding them. To keep the whites white, Momma used "Mrs. Stewart's" bluing in the rinse water. I had heard that some women used that same product to get the blue in their white hair. I wondered it it were true.

My job was to catch the clothes as they came out of the wringer. I was warned about keeping my fingers away from the two rotating cylinders; so I wasn't allowed to put the clothes into the wringer. As the wash water was squeezed out of the clothes, I would catch them from the wringer and shake them to make sure the wrinkles were out and that they were ready to hang. I also carefully loaded them into the wicker basket to be carried outside near the clothes lines. The lines were strung from tree-to-tree in the back yard. As Momma wiped down the wire lines to remove any dirt; my job was to pick up garments and hand them one-by-one to Momma. First would be the whites, then the colored, and then the over-alls. If there wasn't enough room on the line, we'd drape the over-alls over a fence. I also had to be sure that the clip clothes pins were available. I'd hand them to Momma. On this particular day, I was very diligent. After the spilt milk episode, I needed redemption!

After the clothes had been hung to dry, the clean-up was time consuming. The tubs had to be emptied, the washer drained, and the exhaust hose cooled and disconnected. Then the big green washer was wheeled back to its home of the back porch, waiting or another Monday to roll around. We only washed once a week. What a change automatic washers and driers have made on such a household task.

It seemed that every farm woman had the same schedule: Monday was washday, Tuesday was ironing day, Wednesday was Ash Creek Club day, and Thursday and Fridays were called "free" days unless farm produce like cherries, peaches, pears, beans, and tomatoes needed to be canned. If the time was really free for her, she would finish embroidery, sewing, painting, or whatever project she had going. Momma liked crafts. They provided time for her to relax and think private thoughts while she created beautiful crewel embroidery pillows or crocheted wool afghans. I have a lovely crewl embroidered picture and a gold and beige afghan that were products of Momma's loving hands.

Saturday was cleaning day as well as market day. In the morning, we'd dust the furniture and sweep the carpet and floors. We'd have a very light lunch because we knew that we'd get an ice cream soda at Brown's Rexall store. We all got cleaned up and wore our nice clothes. Momma always put on a nice dress. I was never allowed to wear my cover-alls. I had to wear a dress or a skirt and blouse.

Washington was the county seat and the court house was in the town square. Many farmers came for business at the court house in the morning and stayed to meet with neighbors in the afternoon.

The women met and sat in cars that were angle-parked along Main Street. The best parking spot was near the bank corners or in front of Butler's Grocery. Lots of facts and gossip were learned at that time. Momma's best friend, Enid Greenwood, knew all the news. She was what Daddy called, "the town crier". The men did their congregating on the First National Bank corner on Main Street. They, too, indulged in their brand of gossip and crop reports. I recall the Saturday evenings when Momma and Daddy would share the news of the day at the supper table.

We weren't regular church-goers, so Sundays were spent reading the **Topeka Daily Capital** newspapers that had arrived during the week. I liked to make paper doll chains out of the wide sheets of newsprint. Dorothy taught me how to fold the paper and outline a shape. Then I'd cut on the line and open up the strip to reveal people-shaped figures holding hands. That always kept me busy; but it sure made my hands dirty. Then every Sunday, rain or shine, we'd have a big dinner either at our house or down at "the creek" at Grandpa and Grandma's. Sometimes Momma would confess to me that she'd like to have just the five of us for Sunday dinner; but the tradition had been set and she wasn't the one to alter it. George and Mary were good in-laws and they really loved having me around. I enjoyed going to their house because I thought that Grandma made the best chicken and dumplings. She also had "goodies" in the kitchen table drawer for me **if** I ate a good meal. I usually cleaned my plate and got my reward. A Cherry Mash candy bar or a Hershey bar were usually waiting for me.

And so it was, that at the age of four, I learned what the term "spilt milk" really meant. It meant a disregard for Momma's rules; it meant hard work for my brother and me to get the porch clean; it meant that things can't be replaced -- like the five gallons of milk that could not be used by my family and my grandparents. It also reinforced my dislike for milk. Only one good thing about the incident -- it happened on a Monday. It was wash day!

"A Day That Will Live in Infamy"

It was December 7, 1941 -- a regular Sunday with nothing special going on. We weren't church-goers, so after the farm chores were finished, we sat around the house. It was a wonderful time to be together. I can recall that we would read papers that had accumulated during the week. There was no mail delivery on Sunday, so we didn't get a Sunday paper until Monday. The week's worth of reading material kept both Daddy and Momma busy. Daddy liked the sports pages and news about the St. Louis Cardinals while Momma liked the crossword puzzles. Dorothy and I shared the comics.

Jigsaw puzzles were often set up on the library table and we'd gather around to work on them. If a puzzle piece came up missing, not to worry! Daddy would expertly cut one from cardboard and color it to match the scene. (This is where I got my love for puzzles. I have even mastered the art of cutting out cardboad to match the missing pieces -- just like Daddy !)

Sunday dinner was always special; so during our "family time", Momma would be preparing wonderful pies or rolls that produced a mouth-watering aroma throughout the house. The meal that I especially liked was Swiss steak that she made with onions and tomatoes simmered over pieces of round steak. The rich gravy was delicious over creamy whipped mashed potatoes. Yum!

After the dinner dishes were finished by Dorothy and me, we would often go for a Sunday drive. Many times we'd go down to "the creek" to visit Grandpa and Grandma.

Of course, many Sundays found them over at our house. If the weather was gray and cold, we'd gather in the living room and turn on the radio. I found this to be boring as I didn't like the news reports, the stock and weather up-dates, or the classical music that was usually broadcast to enrich our lives. If music didn't have words or a distinct melody, I couldn't sit still and listen to it. I usually amused myself by going outside into the brisk winter air until I was too cold to use my imagination in play; then I'd return inside and sit at my little green desk in the kitchen corner and color in coloring books or scribble messages on note papers. I hadn't started school yet, so "scribble" was the accurate description of my work.

On this particular Sunday, I heard a news announcement that startled both Momma and Daddy. I heard frantic expressions: "Oh, no!" "How could that happen?" "I can't believe it!" "Oh, God! We'll be in war now!" The serious and astonished tones made the afternoon take on a somber air. Being too young to understand the meanings of my parents' phrases, I did know, however, that something awful had happened. I very seldom heard Daddy swear unless he was working on the combine; but today, I felt tension and sensed that my family was affected, just like all the families in the U.S.

In the weeks to come, I'd hear the voices of many broadcasters. I'd later learn the names of FDR, Lowell Thomas, and H.V. Kaltenborn. Pictures from **Life** magazine
showed me a place called Pearl Harbor with the devastation, the billowing clouds of smoke, and the naval ships clustered in a tangled junkyard mess. I also learned a new word -- **war**. I realize now that this horrific event had stolen my naivete and my innocence. It reached around the world and touched this little Kansas farm and this family. It made me scared. Would the war come over here?

I can't recall the details; but I remember that Roy was drafted into the Army. The day he left was such a sad one for all of us. I can remember Momma keeping Roy's room just the way he left it --rumpled bed with an imprint of his head still in the bed pillow. She didn't make up the bed for weeks and I'd often find her in his room looking at the spot where her son had been and she'd be crying.

We got a red, white, and blue bordered flag with a blue star in the center to hang in our front window. It was to show that we had a serviceman in our family. As the war progressed, I saw a flag with a gold star in it instead of blue. "Why don't we have a gold star, Momma? It's a lot prettier." Momma explained that the gold star in Mrs. Hamiltons's window indicated that her son was either missing or killed in action. We certainly didn't want a gold star. The cost of a gold star was paid for by a life. We couldn't lose Roy, and I came to love the looks of the blue star in the banner.

As the war advanced, we followed the action in **Life** magazine and the radio. There were battles in the Pacific and Europe -- places that I didn't know. Roy finished his basic training and came home for a brief furlough before he was to be sent overseas. My, he looked so handsome in his khaki uniform and the hat that folded. He even had a few ribbons on his chest, so he looked like a movie soldier to me. His haricut was very short and I teased him that I did a better barbering job than the Army.

Roy was stationed in England; but he expected to be ordered to the front. Momma worried about the news reports concerning the fighting in Europe. We'd get Roy's letters -- little white photographed copies with some strategic words blocked out. Often the letters would take months to get to us and Momma worried a lot about him. One letter in particular made Momma doubtful. Roy wanted to try to get out of the infantry and into a medical tech job. The only hitch -- he'd have to pass medical technology. "That kid had a terrible time with high school science. How will he ever pass those medical studies? Momma prayed for his success, and low-and-behold, Roy passed the exams and got out of the infantry. Momma and Daddy both said that Roy probably had a very good incentive to study hard. We were all proud of him and so glad that he would not have to march through Europe.

The war changed everything. Things didn't seem the same without Roy and there was a sadness and madness about the world events that made me scared. I learned that the world held some very evil people. Perhaps I should have been shielded from pictures in **Life;** but that weekly printing, along with radio reports, was the only way we could get current news about the war. Whenever I saw pictures of Hitler, the Holocaust, and the war casualties, I realized that there was extreme meanness in the world. Perhaps for that reason my games of playing "Cowboys and Indians" in the tee-pee corn shocks and my fighting imaginary red men were no longer to my liking. I believe I had seen enough killing from the pictures in newspapers and magazines. Instead, I began to play dress-up and pretended to be a movie star. This was my escape. I didn't like war!

Our everyday life changed too. Things were rationed and we were issued stamps in order to buy sugar, canned goods, shoes, etc. Gas was allotted to business men, farmers, and special workers. A special sticker on the windshield showed what rate you had. The black and white signs showed an "A", "B", or "C". Because Daddy needed gas to farm, he was issued a "C" for the car and truck and an "R" for the tractors. "R" meant that the vehicle was not used on the highway. That meant that we didn't take "joy rides" on lovely Sunday afternoons. We all conserved -- stepping on tin cans and recycling them; saving fat and grease for the making of ammunition; using rationing stamps; buying savings stamps for 25 cents each and cashing them in for

War Bonds for $18.75 when the stamp book was filled. I would accompany Momma to the Methodist Church in town and help a ladies' auxiliary wrap gauze bandages and package them for the Red Cross. My job was to carefully take the wrapped rolls over to a counter where a lady would sort them by size and pack them into boxes with big crimson crosses on them.

Sometimes it was hard to give up something. My sister had been invited to the Junior-Senior Prom and she wanted a new pair of shoes to wear with her formal. The floor-length navy blue and white dotted Swiss gown would have looked so pretty with the shoes that Dorothy had selected from the "Monkey Wards" catalogue. (That's what we called the Montgomery Ward store.) There was only one stamp left in Dorothy's War Ration Book and Momma and Daddy said that the style of shoes, although pretty, was too impractical to purchase. She had to remember that she had only one stamp left and the shoes would be needed for everyday school wear. I remember Dorothy dashing upstairs to her room. She was crying and we all felt sorry for her. She seldom asked for anything. I followed her and tried my best to console her. I didn't do much; but I found hankies for her to cry in. She did find a nice pair of shoes that went well with the long dress and they looked good with her school skirts. We did miss the days before rationing when we could buy anything that we could afford.

Life went on during this never-ending war. We were getting baby chicks in for our brooder house. It was June 6, 1944. We had to go to Hadachecks's Hatchery where our order had arrived by train from Clinton, Missouri. The news broke out among the people at the hatchery. "The war is coming to an end!" We all cheered and hugged each other with tears streaming down our faces. When we got home, we tended to our chicks, and then immediately turned on the radio. This time I listened to the newscasters and we all rejoiced. This horrible war was finally ending and Roy would be coming home. Months later, on September 2, 1945, the Japanese would surrender and it would all be over.

Many changes had occurred during war time. From 1941 to 1945, I continued to grow like a skinny weed. I began school and I learned to read, write, and figure math problems. Then our family became smaller when Dorothy was graduated from high school in 1942 and moved to Wichita to take a job at Cessna Aircraft. Daddy bought the Graves' farm and we moved there -- only a half mile south of the Hockenberry house. We were blessed that Roy remained safe and we learned that he had fallen in love with a girl form North Carolina who was a WAC. She later became his bride. We had managed to live well and to be safe -- not like so many others in the world; but we longed for the days when there would be no more fighting and no more rationing. We wanted to return to the "good old days".

Of course it took many months for life to return to normalcy, or some semblance of it. World War II was the biggest event in my memory because it captured a part of my childhood that has never been replaced. As a child, I felt that all people were good; that we could all get along; that God's world was a happy place. That was what I considered "normal" in my innocent way of thinking. The sight of one of our hometown boys from Washington, who had survived a Japanese prison camp, is still etched in my mind as a reminder of how brutal people can be. This poor young man, stick-thin with hollow lifeless eyes and no voice, presented a distorted picture of how I remembered him in his graduation photo. With nothing to do and nowhere to go, he would sit on the sunny First National Bank corner and bask in the Kansas warmth. I felt a mixture of fear and sorrow for him. He was a scary sight to see and I could only imagine the torture that he had endured; yet he was much too weak to pose a threat to me or anyone else. Why was I fearful of him? I guess it was because I didn't know what to say. I could only smile at him and realize that he was someone's son and brother. It could have been Roy if circumstances had been different; so I always said a silent prayer of thanks to God. Momma would often say, "There but for the grace of God go I." Now I understood that saying.

Perhaps if this war hadn't occurred, other events would have shaped me into the pragmatic person that I became. I remember World War II as "the important war" because we were all behind it. All of us, young and old, worked toward the victory. So many other wars and conflicts have happened since; and while I felt compassion, I never felt the deep slash that World War II put on my heart. Was that due to the fact that I never had another loved one in a war? Was I too busy in the process of growing up and going to high school and college to care about another skirmish? (Korean Conflict)

Was I too busy raising children to feel the pain that war brings? (Bay of Pigs) Was it due to the fact that through the years our government has put our military into situations that are not immediately vital to the well-being of our country? (Vietman, Desert Storm, Iraq, and now Afghanistan) Maybe I was simply jaded, thinking of only what I wanted out of life and feeling that we were safe and secure here in our homeland.

Then on 9/11/01, the stomach-churning memory came forward again when the devastation of the Twin Towers in New York and the Pentagon in Washington, D.C. were hit by planes commandeered by terrorists. My first husband and I were watching our youngest grandson, Keith, on this particular Monday when our daughter, Suzanne, called from her work and reported the tragedy to us. I immediately kept Keith in the family room watching a "Veggie Tales" video. He was occupied and having fun. I turned the TV on in the back bedroom and saw the news report and the devastation.

I remembered my fears when Pearl Harbor was struck and I wanted to shield Keith from the type of fear and anxiety that I had experienced some 60 years earlier. In 1941, the news of the attack was verbal; on this day in 2001, the news was both verbal and visual -- too much for a little boy of four to comprehend. I also wanted my son and his wife to explain this horrendous happening to him and to surround him with love and security in his own little family. This episode jolted my thinking. I should never forget the sacrifices of all those service men and women who served for me and my freedom -- not just in World War II, but in all wars and "military skirmishes."

Years earlier when my daughter was scheduled to have hip-replacement surgery to correct the ravages of rheumatoid arthritis, I was making the surgery appointment date. It was to be on December 7. "Oh, that is a day that will live in infamy," I jokingly stated. The young receptionist gave me a blank look. She had absolutely no clue as to what I was referring to. I told her that I was making reference to the beginning of World War II, December 7, 1941. "Oh", was her reply. It meant nothing to her; but it flooded my heart with memories of years past. It reminded me of my lackadaisical attitude throughout years when we had other wars. How dishonorable of me to forget the sacrifices that were made for my freedom. I didn't want to be like this young woman; and yet in her indifference, she was a carbon copy of me!

"Poop-Poop-a-Doop"

Summer on the Kansas farm in 1942 was hot and lonesome for me. I had just turned five in April and was going to start school in September. I was restless and hankering for playmates. Daddy was always busy in the wheat fields; Momma had the responsibility of feeding the harvest work hands and keeping the house neat and tidy in spite of the Kansas dust storms. Both of them had the added burden of worrying about Roy, who was in the Army. Maps of **Life** magazine were marked with the route of Roy's infantry unit and his photo-copied letters were neatly arranged in a slotted letter-holder nearby. It is only now in my adult years, after having sons of my own, that I can comprehend the constant fear and concern that they had in their hearts and minds.

My sister, Dorothy, was twelve years older than I. She helped Momma with the cooking, cleaning, and tending after me. I probably was a big nuisance to her; but she never let on. In fact, she shared movie star pictures with me. Whenever she had a new **Photoplay**, she'd cut out new pictures for her wall décor and give me the old ones that she had replaced. I pasted them in a scrapsbook -- Lana Turner, Alice Faye, Barbara Stanwyck, Alan Ladd, Robert Taylor, and Clark Gable. My favorite had always been Clark Gable; while Dorothy liked Robert Taylor.

Dorothy was someone for me to envy. She was pretty with a "peaches and cream" complexion and she was an accomplished cook and a good student. Her patience and kind temperament helped her endure the tricks that I used to play on her. While we were not close in age, we were bonded by family ties. I never considered her my "half-sister"; she was my whole sister all the way. Because of the age difference, we never played and had things in common as kids do when they're with their peers. That changed, however, when I became an adult and the age difference was not as extreme. Perhaps our closest time together was when we traveled to the Holy Land in 2006. It was a journey of love.

My nearest girl friend, Merle Gauby, lived a couple of miles away; so when we got together to play, it had to be arranged. That meant that I used my imagination and played with my dolls and my devoted dog Rags. They became a substitute for a real "girl pal". I would recall stories from Momma about her childhood girl friends in St. Louis. It must have been wonderful to live in a big city with people all around -- especially girlfriends who lived next door.

Sunday afternoon was usually a day of rest for all of us. Daddy didn't do field work unless it was absolutely necessary; so that meant the chores of milking the cows, gathering the eggs, and feeding the pigs and chickens made it an easy day. Dorothy would often make a batch of her famous fudge. She was the best candy maker around, and we would finish a plate of fudge in an afternoon. While we were indulging ourselves in caloric suicide, we would get out Momma's photo albums of her earlier life in St. Louis. Those big, black-paged books, with gold-embossed leaves on the leather bindings, held memories of Momma's youth and visions of a life that I envied. The sepia photos revealed that Momma was pretty -- Momma was silly -- Momma was popular! That was what I wanted for myself; but at the age of five, I was a scrawny, freckled-faced lonesome kid in cover-alls.

Two of Momma's best friends were Georgina and Beatrice. Both were pretty Gibson Girl types. What fun they had as the scenes showed them on porch swings eating ice cream cones, or making funny poses and showing off in swim suits that covered everything except the ankles! How schocking!

As the years passed, the friends kept in touch. There were many envelopes holding letters and greeting cards. It was fun to read the sentiments. Georgina remained in St. Louis with her family, but died suddenly when she was in her early twenties. Momma never knew the cause of her death. Perhaps it was appendicitis, like the situation that had claimed her mother's life. Momma had married her first husband and had moved to Kansas City when she heard of Georgina's passing. I remember hearing Momma recall that when she heard the sad news, she wondered why anyone so young should die. A year later Momma's husband died suddenly, leaving her a widow with the challenge of raising a son and a daughter. Again she thought, "He's too young" -- but Momma realized that death can come when you least expect it

-- after all, she had lost her mother, a best friend, and now her husband. Only God knows when the final hour will be. Momma knew that life goes on, and she did just that -- becoming a practical nurse and later marrying my father and creating a new life for herself and her children.

With Georgina gone, Momma kept closer contact with Beatrice, or "Bea", as she was called. I remember seeing beautiful greeting cards arriving at Easter, Thanksgiving, Christmas, and birthdays. Some of them bore postmarks from foreign countries with stamps that were too pretty to throw away. As a kid, I didn't know about stamp collecting; but I cut the stamps off the envelopes and glued them into a spiral notebook for safe keeping. Bea also sent us many photographs of herself and her husband, Val. He was a tall, handsome, military man with a chest full of medals. Scenes from many big cities showed the couple smiling and enjoying a luxurious life. Bea was often wearing fur stoles, hats with feathers and veils, bracelets over kid gloves, and high heels that accentuated her shapely legs. That's when Bea got the name of "Poop-Poop a Doop" from my father and brother. Both of them thought that she was pretty, but very pretentious. Of course that nickname was used only around the house; and Daddy would tease Momma about having such a fancy girlfriend. In fact, Momma marveled at the fact that "Little Bea" had married so well. She was just a poor little kid from St. Louis; but she had always been smart and eager to learn. Momma got a thrill knowing that Bea was traveling and experiencing so many worldly adventures. Bea's letter and cards always were a welcome diversion for Momma. Although she never showed it, maybe Momma was a little envious -- especially when she had to kill and dress chickens for a big harvest meal. It would be so much nicer to be lunching in an open-air café or traveling to the mountains; but life here on the Kansas farm was good. She could envision Bea's adventures as she plucked each feather one-by-one.

After looking at some of Bea's photos from the album, Daddy walked over to Momma and put his arms around her as she was putting the albums away. "Maybe I ought to buy you some fancy duds, Clara. You'd look every bit as good as Bea. Maybe better!"

Momma straightened the collar on her plaid cotton shirtwaist dress and looked up lovingly at Daddy. "Oh, Carl, don't be silly. How could I get any work done around here in that fancy garb? And come to think of it, I don't think you could find a fur coat around here unless you set a trap for it." We all laughed at the idea.

Perhaps my Daddy wished that he could afford the grand clothes for Momma. Of course they would be impractical for life on the farm; but I remember a birthday gift that he gave her one year. It was a lovely of mother-of-pearl locket with a gold embossed leaf on the front. The leaf design was reminiscent of the leaf pattern on the old photo album. I have no idea how much the gold necklace cost; but seeing the velvet jeweler's box and the tears in Momma's eyes when she put the chain around her neck; it probably made a dent in the proceeds from the recent wheat harvest. Inside the locket, Momma cut two small photos of Daddy and Roy. "My two best men," she proudly exclaimed. She wore this locket every evening when she'd change from her "work" housedress into something fresh, because "Carl will be coming in from the field soon." As a child, I thought the locket made Momma as pretty as "Poop-Poop a Doop", and I think it made Momma feel that way too.

One hot July morning, I ran down to the mailbox with Rags following close behind. On either side of the road, there was a line of gravel about eight inches deep. When the county road grader came by every week or so, the gravel would be re-distributed to keep the entire surface covered with tiny crushed rocks. Because of this, I was always getting gravel and grit in my sandals. I had to stop several times to remove the annoying stones. The mailbox wasn't far from our front porch; but it took me several minutes to sit down by the roadside, remove my sandals, shake the grit out, and put them on again. Momma always told me to wear my leather "Buster Brown" laced shoes when I went outside; but they were too much trouble to tie. My ability to buckle far out-weighed my ability to tie.

When I opened the mail box, I was pleased to see several letters and cards along with the daily paper. One letter stood out amid all the others. It was a photo-copied letter like the ones we'd get from Roy. Someone from overseas was writing to us. The hand writing had twists and twirls that designated that the writer was probably female. My heart raced. The writing looked a lot like the old letters from "Poop-Poop a Doop" that was tucked away in the albums. Oh, I hoped my observation was right! It had only been recently that we had thumbed through the albums-- now here she was again.

I hurriedly ran back to the house. This time I didn't stop to remove my sandals to get the rocks out. I endured the pain. I cast all the other mail aside and put the small black and white letter in Momma's hand. I couldn't wait for Momma to open the envelope and confirm that this indeed was a letter from "Poop-Poop a Doop".

Momma looked at the note. Some vital words had been censored; but she was able to decipher that Bea and her husband would be returning to the States in September. "It's been a long time since I've seen you and I hope to visit you soon. I'll write more when I get to New York." Those were the only words that were not blacked out. War time had meant that foreign correspondence was often censored. Since Bea's husband was in the

Air Corps, the purpose of his trip had been blocked out. My mother couldn't believe her eyes as she read and re-read the note.

When Daddy came in for the noon meal, I greeted him with the news: "Poop-Poop a Doop" is coming to visit us." I repeated it over and over in a sing-song voice until Momma told me to, "Hush"; and she proceeded to relay the news to Daddy. As he took the Lava soap and lathered his hands and arms, he smiled. "That's wonderful. I know you'll enjoy seeing her after all these years. How long will she be able to stay? Is she coming in on the bus, or can we pick her up somewhere?" That day the lunch conversation centered on the future visit. We were all excited; but we'd have to wait for a letter from state-side.

As the days passed, I kept a close eye on the mailman. I was eager to get the letter that would give us the exact information about the upcoming visit. All through July and August, I kept a vigil on the mail box, only to be disappointed time after time. Then on the first day of September, there it was -- a beautiful lavender envelope that had the fullness to it that indicated that photos were probably inside. I could make out the New York postmark and I recognized her beautiful hand writing. My little tan legs ran as fast as my heart was beating.

"Momma, Momma! It's a letter from "Poop-Poop a Doop"!" I grabbed the letter opener and handed it to Momma. We felt a sense of excitement as she opened the envelope, took out the lavender sheets along with two photos, and began to read aloud:

Dear Clara.
    Val and I will be coming to the Midwest in late September. Val has military work to assume at the base in Lincoln, Nebraska. Since you live only 90 miles from there, I can't pass up the chance to visit. I'll have a car at my disposal and I'll plan to drive down early in the morning of September 25, spend the day, and return later in the day. I hope this is not an imposition on you. Don't worry about directions for me. Val has a grid map and he knows just where your farm is located. He'll write out a map for me. I really look forward to seeing you again, Clara. I've always kept you in my heart and I want so much to meet your family.

                        See you soon,
                        Bea

While Momma had been reading, I was studying the two black and white photos that had been enclosed. In one photo Val and Bea were seated at an outdoor café. My! There were so many glasses on the table. What were they drinking? The second photo was a close-up of Bea in an evening gown with a large corsage on her shoulder. On the back she had written, "Taken in our villa in Naples."

I waited until Momma had finished re-reading the note and then I asked: "Momma,

What's a villa? Where's Naples?" Before she could answer, I studied the pictures again. Bea was pretty and glamorous -- almost like a movie star. I wondered if Momma would let me have that picture to add to my movie scrapbook?

During the next three weeks, the house became a bee-hive of activity. Momma always believed in spring and fall house-cleaning; so it stood to reason that we'd be doing some heavy cleaning in order to welcome our guest. The walls would be dusted, the woodwork washed with "Spic and Span", the draperies aired, and the sheer curtains washed. Dorothy and I were assigned to wash and wax the linoleum floor in the kitchen. That was always a fun job -- or at least I thought so. Dorothy did all the mopping; but later I would help rub in the paste wax. We'd get an old ragged winter coat that was used for the buffing and I'd sit on it while Dorothy pulled me around to buff the wax shine. As I glided around the floor on the old coat, the cream colored linoleum with its blue flower-block design came to life and took on a rich, shiny luster.

Even Daddy took time from farm duties to participate in the cleaning routine. He rolled up the carpets in the living room and the bedroom, took them outside on the clothes line and beat the tar (dust) out of them. This was before electricity came to the farm, so cleaning was a very tedious task. We didn't have the power vacuums that we have today. It was even Daddy's idea to put two new "walking boards" down as a walkway from the house to the driveway. The old boards were warped and splintered -- not at all suitable for a lady in high heels. We were really "pulling out the stops" for our expected guest.

As the appointed day drew nearer and nearer and the house became cleaner and cleaner, I found myself becoming worried. Would she be as pretty as her picutres showed? Would she be "stuck up"? Would she like me? What would I say to her? How would she accept our humble farm house and the outdoor toilet? Somehow these questions that were whirling around in my head made me sad and withdrawn. Momma realized this because one night, as we sat on the porch watching the night sky, she asked me about my feelings. She beckoned me to sit on her lap, and I confessed all my worries and doubts to her.

"Don't worry about any of those things. Bea is a lot like me. We grew up together in St. Louis, didn't have a lot of money or fancy things, and didn't really know much about the world. Bea did all right and I know she has seen sights that I can only imagine; but deep down, she's still my childhood friend from St. Louis. Nothing will ever change that. I know you'll like her and I'm certain she'll love you. Did you know that she has a daughter?" I shook my head "no". "Well, she does -- and her daughter's name is Rosemary, just like yours." Momma gave me a hug before I slipped off her lap. Not once did she mention that I should not refer to Bea as "Poop-Poop a Doop". I felt better.

September 25 finally arrived. I woke up earlier than usual and put on my favorite blue cotton dress with red rick-rack trim. I also put on my new shoes. All the kids at school liked this outfit, so I imagined Bea would like it too. I was thankful that this was a weekend and I didn't have to go to school. I gobbled down my breakfast and then ran upstairs to look out the front bedroom window that had a spectacular view of the road. I could see for at least a mile and even farther if I noticed a dust cloud being stirred up by a car or truck. It was a long vigil and several cars approached, getting my hopes up, only to pass by the house. Then around ten o'clock I noticed dust being stirred by a car that began to slow down as it got nearer and nearer. "I think she's coming!" I yelled down the stairs. When the car pulled into the drive, I bolted down the steps. "She's here! She's here!" Momma took off her apron, Daddy put down the newspaper, and Dorothy and I blended into the background. I was excited, yet nervous.

Bea stopped at the plank walk-way. She turned her head to the left to see Momma running down the porch steps with arms out-stretched. Bea opened the door and got out to be embraced by her childhood friend. I had only seen Momma embrace family members, never strangers -- but then this was no stranger. There she was: "Poop-Poop a Doop".

Momma introduced us all to Bea. I was in awe of this lady; but when she told me to call her "Bea" and not "Mrs. Hawkenson"; I knew that I was really going to like her. She told me about her daughter who shared my name. I felt an immediate bond.

She wore a navy blue dress with a beautiful white lace collar and a white sweater draped over her shoulders. I remember the white color because I could never keep white clothes clean on the farm and I thought this was the fanciest part of her outfit. The white color also accentuated her auburn hair. Later I was to notice a beautiful gold bracelet that held many charms. One in particular fascinated me. Bea told me that it was a figure of the Eiffel Tower in France. There was a hole in the bottom and if you held it up to the light you could see a picture of the Tower in Paris. I was enthralled with it and Bea let me look at it over and over again. She also told me about going to the top of the Tower and seeing the beautiful array of lights. "Paris is known as 'the City of Lights'", she explained. Gee, I had never heard of Paris or France! I knew that I'd have to get an atlas and look up those places.

Another thing about Bea -- she was easy to talk to. She was just like Momma in many ways -- friendly, smiling, and relaxed. I felt that I had known her all of my life. Maybe I had because I knew her from her photos and cards from past years. I could tell that she really liked us and we spent a wonderful September day together. Momma had set up a great lunch with my favorite pressed chicken sandwiches, home grown tomatoes, and cherry cobbler. Bea commented on how everything was so good. "I can bet that it's all home-grown." --and it was.

After lunch, Dorothy and I cleaned up. It was time for Momma and Bea to have a private visit. The two of them sat in the living room and reminisced about growing up in St. Louis, getting married, and now renewing an old friendship. We heard snippets of laughter and a few sobs now and then.

After hours of visiting, Momma and Bea joined the rest of us on the porch. We decided to finish the rest of the cobbler and enjoy some iced tea. The afternoon had flown by and it was nearing the time for Bea to leave and return to Lincoln. Bea had told her husband to expect her return to be around eight in the evening. The sun was sinking in the west. It was bringing closure to a day that I had anticipated for so long. Now it was almost over. That's the way it is with life -- you look forward and dream of something and then "pouf" it's over in an instance. Before she walked to the car, I asked to take one more glance at the Eiffel Tower charm.

"Of course you may, Rosemary." She stooped down and extended her wrist. I noticed a wonderful floral scent about her.

"You sure smell pretty," I whispered.

"That's a perfume called "Joy". Here, I have a little falcon in my purse. Let me put some behind your ears." Oh, how tickled I was!

Momma and Bea posed for a picture and then embraced, wondering if they would ever see each other again. We all waved our good-byes as Bea slowly pulled out of the drive onto the gravel road. Momma wiped tears from her eyes and I secretly touched behind my ears to release the floral scent of "Joy". Then I ran upstairs to follow Bea's car as long as my eyes could make out the car's image in the dusky evening.

That day had been a very special one for me. I had learned so much. First of all, I learned that fancy clothes don't make the person. It was what was inside a person that mattered. Calling this beautiful lady "Poop-Poop a

Doop" seemed so unfair now that I had met a genuine person who was not pretentious at all. Momma was right. Bea was a lot like her; they were both real from the inside out. From then on, whenever thoughts of her came to my mind, I always referred to her as "Bea".

The second thing that I learned was to keep your friends throughout a life-time, if you can. I learned that friends are precious and are not to be casually discarded. Momma and Bea had kept in touch, even though their lifestyles were so opposite. Bea had traveled extensively while Momma stayed put. Yet, a common bond held them together -- love.

Would I keep in touch with my girlfriends through the years? Maybe I wouldn't be as fortunate; but I could always look back on this day and remember two girlfriends who did.

Another lesson learned was the location of France and the Eiffel Tower. I told the kids about that when I returned to school the next day. I also let my girlfriends smell the perfume behind my ears. They were so envious and wanted to know where they could get some for their mothers. "Paris, France," I boastfully replied. I knew that they didn't have a clue as to where that was!

As the years passed, Bea and Clara continued to exchange Christmas and birthday cards yearly. This September day was the last time, however, that they were ever to see each other. Now my parents and Bea have passed on; but when I capture the fragrance of "Joy", I remember that gorgeous autumn day, the lovely visitor, and the life lessons that have served me well. All this was because two lovely ladies were not only childhood friends, but lifetime friends.

Bea and Momma

A Biting Word

Every farm usually had a dog or two along with barn cats that we called "mousers". I always had the companionship of a dog while I was growing up. I learned early about their loyalties and unconditional love. Over the years there were "Godlip", "Rags", "Rover", "Tippy, "Jiggs," and "Mickey" in my portfolio of canine friends. The last three were Boston bull terriers that Momma acquired over the years and kept in the house. The others were outside dogs until the weather became cold and unbearable -- then they got to stay on the porch or inside a utility closet that we dubbed "Godlip's Room" because he was the first to occupy it. The outside dogs kept watch over the property and warned us of any trespassers, as well as welcoming friendly visitors. The loud barks drew our attention. Their racket was our farm door bell!

We discouraged the dogs from getting too near the road. The gravel was usually too deep for their paws to feel comfortable, and most of them obeyed. Old Godlip was the exception. He would dart out in a minute to bite the small front tires of a Farm-all tractor. He was a mix of a black lab and a pit bull. Sometimes I'd find him sitting forlornly on the front porch with the imprints of the small front tires of the tractor over his shoulder. He hated wheels and he would bark and try to attack every tractor that passed by. The farmers didn't hit him on purpose. He just wouldn't get out of their way. As vicious as he was to tractors; he was a gentle giant to me. I would roll around the porch floor with him, get on his back and ride him, and even put doll bonnets on him. He was too big for doll clothes; but I tried to dress him. He took all this playing until he got tired -- then he'd walk away toward the barn and hide behind the milk stanchions.

When Godlip passed away from natural causes (not from a tractor incident), we were all sad. Then within a week, Rags somehow came into our lives. He was only a pup, so we assumed that someone tossed him out along the road. Farmers often got unwanted animals that way. It's a cruel thing to do; but this little pup found just the right home at just the right time. He didn't replace Godlip in our hearts; he was merely added to the list of best dog friends in my life. I feel that you never forget anyone or any animal that you have truly loved. Perhaps this eternal memory is another form of eternal life.

Rags was what my Grandpa called a "pickle dog" -- a Heinz 57 breed. Rags looked like a sheltie, but he was a little bit bigger. His face had white markings; but his coat was many shades of brown and tan with flecks of white and gray throughout. He looked like a pile of rags, hence the name, "Rags". He had a peculiar way of showing his teeth as if he were about to snap. This scared many people until they got to know him. He was a gentle and obedient dog. I referred to the showing of his teeth as his "smile". Since he slept on the side porch and guarded the entry door to the kitchen, I imagine he scared away many a salesman when they saw his toothy "smile."

He was always ready to play with me in the yard and fields. I'd toss sticks for him to retrieve. I'd chase him around the shocks of corn that stood like Indian teepees, I'd dodge in and out of the shocks to try to confuse him; but he'd always find me and jump up to kiss my face and "smile" at me. I loved that dog!

Rags would always follow me to the corner mail box. Even though the gravel hurt his paws, he'd be right by my side. When a car or truck would be traveling by, he'd stay very close to me until the vehicle passed. He was not aggressive to tires like Godlip had been. He was my protector. If I walked, he'd walk; if I ran, he'd run. Momma thought he should have been called "Shadow" instead of Rags because he followed me everywhere.

One day as we were playing in the yard, our neighbor, Minnie Bell, was walking down the road. Minnie was a tiny woman who always wore a long dress, apron, and sunbonnet. I don't think the sun's rays ever touched her skin. Minnie was not a favorite person of mine because I had heard my parents talk about how stingy she was. Kids hear a lot from the kitchen table discussions. Even at the age of five, I became very bigoted towards Minnie.

Daddy farmed her land and he always wanted to fertilize the crops to get a better yield. Minnie never wanted to pay her share. That angered Daddy and I would overhear him tell Momma that Minnie wanted the money that a good yield would produce, but she didn't want to pay. One day when she was at the house, she moaned, "How am I going to pay my taxes?" I blurted out, "That's not our problem!" Needless to say, Momma whisked me out of the kitchen. The saying, "Little pitchers have big ears" was true in my case. I also had a big mouth.

One summer afternoon, Dorothy and I were in the upstairs bedroom with the windows wide open. We heard shouts coming from Minnie's pasture across the road. Being curious, we ran to the open window to see Minnie taking a dead tree branch and hitting her crippled husband, Charley, on the back. She was yelling,"Get those cows in the barn.", "Get going!" And some other words that we couldn't decipher, while she continued to hit him. After seeing that scene played out in the pasture, she seemed like a witch to me. I didn't like her, even though she hadn't done anything sinister to me. How could someone hit a crippled old man who wasn't able to move very fast? I really didn't know Charley, but I felt sorry for him. He kept to himself while Minnie did all the business.

Rags took notice of Minnie walking along the gravel road. Since she was covered from head to foot in sun-shielding garb, she made a funny-looking figure. Rags began to bark at her as she approached. I didn't stop Rags; but instead I yelled out: "Cigar her, cigar her." I must have heard the word "sic" in a western movie at the Major Theater in town or when Daddy was herding cows. I knew that it meant to charge at the object; but I felt that I wasn't using "that" word. I was using another word that kinda sounded like "sic". Surely Rags would know the difference. He was a smart dog.

As Minnie came nearer to the side of our yard, I continued to chant "Cigar her!" Rags followed my command and took after Minnie and nipped her just above the heel. I was shocked that he would actually bite someone. I never thought that the word "cigar" would get the same response as "sic". I was scared and ashamed at what I had done; but I wasn't brave enough to apologize to Minnie and to see if she needed medical aid. I ran! Rags ran with me to the porch and we crawled under the breeze-way. The dirt floor, spider webs, and daddy long legs made for an uncomfortable hiding place. I hugged Rags and told him I was so sorry that I had commanded him to do a bad thing. I peeked through the wooden lattice and watched as Minnie got her mail and walked back to her house. Thank goodness she didn't stop in to speak to my parents. Maybe she was going to ignore what had happened. Rags and I hid out until Momma called me to lunch.

"Rosemary, it's lunch time," Momma shouted out not realizing that I was very close-by under the porch. When Rags and I crawled out, I was covered with dirt and cobwebs. Momma was not at all pleased with my appearance.

"What have you been doing under the porch all morning? What a mess you are! You need to change your clothes and wash up before you come to the table, young lady." When she called me "young lady", I knew she was very upset with me.

Momma had every right to be disgusted with me. Lunch was on the table and now she had to contend with me. I knew that both Momma and Daddy would be very disappointed with me when they learned the news about Minnie. I couldn't find the courage to confess what I had done and what I had urged Rags to do. Rags wasn't at fault; I was! I had heard about mean dogs that bit people and had to be destroyed; but Rags wasn't mean. I didn't want something bad to happen to him. My stomach was in knots and I felt hot tears coming to my eyes. I hardly touched my meal, even though it was one of my favorites, fried chicken. Momma, being the good mother, thought that I was coming down with something. She felt my forehead for a sign of fever. I kept my eyes downward and didn't say a word. I was coming down with something all right, it was called cowardliness.

After lunch I plopped down on my bed. I wanted to disappear; I wanted to start the day over again. How could I have been so stupid? My head ached and I didn't feel well at all. Then I thought about Rags. He sensed that he had done something wrong, yet he had followed my orders. I got up and went out to the yard to find him. As always, he was waiting for me. He was still my buddy and my friend. I needed to apologize to him and hoped to make things better. I ruffled his fur and gave him a hug. Rags "smiled", licked the tears that were streaming down my cheeks, and forgave me. Now if only I could forgive myself.

Something told me to take Rags and go to the back yard where I had set up a play house. In the "L" shaped corner of the house, I had set up orange crates, apple baskets, and old dishes and bottles that Momma had discarded. I pretended that it was a home, a café, a candy store, or a hospital. Today it was to be a candy store. A recent rain had made the mud crack in "fudge-like" consistency. I'd cut out squares, put them on plates, and pretend to sell the candy to my dolls and my imaginary customers. We were back there for several hours. Rags was sprawled out on the shady grass and ignored my conversation with my dolls and "customers". I was busy serving candy and taking orders, when all of a sudden my make-believe world was jarred into reality.

"Rosemary, Rosemary! Come in the house right now!" Momma's voice had a sense of urgency to it. There was also an icy tone that made my heart sink. I knew that my secret had been revealed. Oh, I hoped Minnie hadn't called on the telephone to announce this dilemma. We were on a party line and now the whole neighborhood would be in on this news. Our ring was "two longs" and "two shorts". Anyone hearing that ring would know that Carl and Clara were getting a call. Since it was a close-knit community, it wasn't unusual for the neighbors to pick up the receiver and "rubber neck". That was how information traveled in those days. If you had serious business to discuss, you didn't talk about it on the phone because then everyone would know it. I could just imagine that Mrs. Gauby, Mrs. Rogers, Mrs. Nemitz, and Mrs. Whoglemuth had heard "the news about Rosemary".

I told Rags to "stay" as I meekly walked around the house and up the porch steps. I opened the screen door and entered the kitchen. Seated around the table to greet me were Minnie, Daddy, and Momma. When I saw Minnie, I felt a little relief. Perhaps she hadn't called, but had walked up the road to talk to my parents personally. It was good that Rags had been in the back yard with me. At least Minnie didn't have to encounter him again; and he didn't have to meet her, either.

I hung my head in shame waiting for a reprimand. That was the first time that I recognized the inner voice that all of us have -- a conscience! I didn't feel easy with that turmoil that boiled inside me. I was no longer an innocent little girl. I was guilty -- a bad person --a bad seed! Minnie had every right to take a tree branch and hit me, just as she had hit Charley.

Daddy had been called in from his work in the garage. He still had on his leather gloves. Usually when he sat at the table, he had washed. Today there was no smell of Lava soap, just the smell of gasoline, grease, and sweat. Momma still had her apron tied around her waist and a damp dish towel hung from the pocket. She, too, had been interrupted from her after-lunch clean up.

Daddy was the first to speak. "Mrs. Bell tells us that you siced the dog on her this morning as she was walking to the mailbox. She said that Rags nipped her on the right leg just above the heel. What do you have to say about this?"

I bent my head down and felt hot tears stream from my eyes. There was a terrible silence and I knew that they were waiting for my reply. I wanted to run; but I knew that I had to face the consequences. I wiped my nose on my sleeve (something that Momma hated) and rubbed the back of my hands over my eyes to collect the tears. With all the "dirt fudge" that I had made, I knew that I wouldn't dare use my fingers to wipe away the tears. "Yes, I did it", I meekly stated. I couldn't look at them in the face and I bent my head downward and stared into my lap

"You need to look up and face us, Rosemary. And you need to apologize to Mrs. Bell." Momma had placed her fingers under my chin and gently forced my tear-stained face upward.

When I faced Minnie, I saw a tiny, frail old woman who had been a victim of my malicious action. She was only walking on the road to the mailbox to get her mail. She had every right to do that. My guilty conscience was whirling around and around inside my brain, my heart, and my stomach. I felt sick. I knew that I was at fault. Again, I wiped away the tears and wiped my nose on my sleeve. With a fairly dry face, I looked into her steel gray eyes, and uttered an apology through a mouth that felt as if it were full of cotton. "I'm sorry, Mrs.Bell. I didn't think Rags would do that. I only said 'cigar'".

"You were wrong in yelling at anyone walking along the road -- especially a neighbor whom you know. And to use words that sound like an attack command are definitely bad. I can't imagine what you were thinking -- or if you were thinking!" Daddy shook his head and slowly removed his leather work gloves. Then he turned his attention to Minnie. "Tell us what we can do, Minnie. How bad is the bite? Did you see a doctor?"

"It really isn't a bad bite, Carl. See, the dog only ripped my stocking." She shyly raised her long skirt and pointed to the back of her right leg. There were bite marks and snags in her tan cotton stocking. "There are bruises on the skin; but he didn't draw blood. I didn't go to Doc Huntley. I think it's OK." She paused for a moment and then said words that tore at my heart. "I don't like that dog of yours and I want you to get rid of him."

"I can understand that, Minnie. I'll pay for new stockings, a doctor bill, and any medicine you might need for it. I'll also take care of the dog; and I'll have a good talk with my daughter." With that, Daddy grabbed his gloves as a signal that the episode was over.

Momma asked Minnie if she wanted her to look at the wound. After all, Momma was a practical nurse and knew about first-aid treatment. Minnie declined the offer; but she accepted a cool drink before she left the house to walk back to her home. I heard muffled words as Momma and Daddy walked her down the driveway.

I sat in silence at the kitchen table. Daddy went back to his garage workshop; Momma came back and finished her kitchen cleaning. I wondered what would happen next. Poor Rags, he was going to have to be "gotten rid of". "Your daddy and I will talk to you later this afternoon. We have some decisions to make and we need to think things over. I'm sorry this happened and I know you are too -- but you'll learn to watch your words. I think I'm more disappointed by the fact that you didn't tell us about all of this right after it happened. I'm thankful that the bite wasn't too deep. Now run along." Momma had to think about all that had happened and she didn't want me around.

When I left the kitchen to return to my "fudge shop", there was Rags waiting for me. He had no idea what had happened. He had no idea that he was going to have to go to another home. I sat by him the rest of the afternoon, just petting and talking to him. I felt so guilty -- I still do!

The afternoon dragged on. I closed my "fudge shop" early and lolled around on the cool grass. I noticed that Momma had walked down to the workshop to talk with Daddy. I suppose they were mulling over what my punishment should be and what to do with Rags. Minnie's words, "Get rid of that dog", played over and over in my mind. No immediate decision had been made; but I knew that Daddy would be true to his word and he would see that Rags was no longer on our farm. I think Momma and Daddy were stalling a little just to let me stew in my juices of guilt.

Late in the afternoon, Daddy closed his workshop and came up to the house. After he had washed, he called out to me, "Rosemary, get washed and let's go down to Grandpa's." Oh, boy! Now Grandpa and Grandma would have to learn of my mistake.

Grandpa's farm, also known as "the creek", was 2 ½ miles from our house. Usually when I drove with Daddy, he'd sing or whistle songs. His favorites were "Beautiful Brown Eyes" and "I Told Them all about You". Today the ride was done in silence and the trip seemed to be a hundred miles long. Of course, I had never traveled that far. The lane that curved and led to the house was pure sand and it made a muffled sound as the car tires left deep treads. We were incapsulated in silence and I didn't like it. Grandpa's farm was on the banks of Ash Creek and the land was very fertile and produced lush crops of corn, milo, watermelons, and cantaloupes. Daddy did most of the heavy farming; but Grandpa worked during the harvest season. As we reached the house, Grandpa and Grandma came to the kitchen door to greet us. It seemed as if they were expecting us.

"Hey, Carl. Hi, Rosemary! Mary told me that you called. What's this all about" Anything the matter?" Gramdpa was a bundle of inquiries. It wasn't unusual for Daddy to make a daily trek to his parents' farm. Since this was his second trip, no wonder Grandpa was curious.

My grandparents spoiled me. I was their only biological grandchild and they thought that I was perfect. They were about to learn the horrible truth about me and that made me sad all over again. When would this misery ever stop?

Grandpa George was a tall, lean man with thinning white hair and sky blue eyes. When we would be in the harvest field waiting for the combine to unload its cache of grain, we'd sing songs and play games while we sipped Pepsi Cola. I liked to call him my "Blue-eyed Pick-a-Pie". That was a little jingle that we had composed. No one had ever heard of it -- it was ours alone to sing. He walked very upright and it was difficult to detect his arthritis until you looked at his hands. Both hands were deformed by the ravages of the disease. He had difficulty writing and gripping anything. Because of the stiffness, his hands seemed very coarse and it was impossible to hold hands with him.

Grandma Mary was about five feet tall with short bobbed hair that was straight as an arrow. At one time she had grown it down to her shoe tops; but as she aged, she found the short cut much easier to manage and much cooler, too. She was an excellent cook. Her chicken and dumplings, cherry pie, and lime Kool Aid were among my favorites. As all grandmas do, she always had something that I liked around the house. "Look in the table drawer, Rosemary." I'd open it and find a Cherry Mash candy bar or a packet of Wrigley's spearmint gum in tinfoil wrappers. She also liked to read stories to me. "Little Black Sambo" was our favorite short story followed by **The Wizard of Oz.**. When **The Wizard of Oz** was made into a movie, we saw it at the Major Theater in Washington. That was the first film in color that I had ever seen. In fact, I believe it was one of the first Technicolor films produced. It began in black and white and when Dorothy and Toto got to Oz, it was in magnificent color. Another film that we both liked was **Song of the South** and the song "Zip-a-Dee-Doo-Dah" was one that she always sang after seeing the movie. When I hear it today, I think of her.

When we got out of the car, we went to the side of the house near the cave door. There were several metal lawn chairs and a couple of wooden rocking chairs arranged in a semi-circle on the concrete slab. Grandma offered us lemonade; but Daddy declined the offer and said that he wanted to talk. Besides, Clara was fixing supper at home. Daddy told the whole account of what had happened. As he told the story, I picked at the peeling paint on the arm of the rocking chair as I swayed slowly back and forth. When the whole story had been told, Grandpa beckoned to me. "Come over here and sit on my lap, Rosemary."

I reluctantly got up from the rocker, and with head hung down, I sat on Grandpa's lap. His overall bib was always filled with interesting things; but today was not the day to peek into the pockets and find his wallet, pen, pocket knife, tooth pick, pocket watch, and Skoal. This was a time to be quiet.

"You know, Rosemary, we're so sad that all of this happened. I know Rags is a good dog, and I know that you are a good girl. Sometimes we all say things that we don't really mean. You didn't mean to hurt Minnie, and Rags was only following your command. I think that you have learned a lesson today, maybe we all have. Words can bite. They can hurt people; and remember anything with teeth can bite. I bet Rags never bites another person as long as he lives; and I bet you never sic a dog on another person -- no matter what word you use."

I was beginning to feel better, especially when he said that I was a "good girl". Then Grandpa said something that made me glad all over. "You know, Rosemary, I need a dog around here. Dusty died last year and we never found another dog. What do you think about Rags coming here to live with Grandma and me? Would that be OK with you? How about it, Mary? What do you think?" Grandpa's blue eyes had a mischievous twinkle about them as he looked over at Grandma, who smiled in agreement.

Daddy was a little too quick to pick up on the idea. It was not a surprise to him. I bet they had talked about this rescue plan on the phone before we made the trip. "Hey, Dad, that's a great idea and I know you and Rags get along fine. We'll have to be gentle with him for a couple of weeks so that he doesn't want to return home to Rosemary; but he minds very well and I think things will work out. Since I make a trip down here every day, Rosemary can come along and play with the old fella. Let's get him down here tomorrow morning before Minnie picks up her mail." With that, Daddy winked at me and said, "Let's go home. Momma probably has supper waiting for us."

This time the trip home was one of conversation. Daddy and I talked about the event of the day. He confided in me that perhaps he and Momma should have controlled their negative words about Minnie whenever I was within earshot. He told me that as I grew, I would have to be responsible for all of my actions. I would have to pay the consequences and perhaps those I loved would be affected, too. Poor Rags was losing a home and a playmate; but there was another loving home waiting for him. He was lucky -- and so was I, this time. "Momma and I love you, Rosemary. We want you to always know that." We turned onto our drive and were greeted by "smiling" Rags.

And so it was that Rags had a new home with Grandpa and Grandma. I went down to see him everyday when Daddy drove down to "the creek". He never strayed from Grandpa's place. I think he had it too good down there; living a retired life instead of playing with a rowdy five year old. I really missed him; but a change had to be made and this was the best plan for us both. As the years passed, Rags became more and more devoted to Grandpa and Grandma. That was good because I couldn't see him every day when I entered school.

As for Minnie, I tried to avoid her; but I'd wave to her whenever I saw her pass by on the way to the mailbox. I had no more "biting words" for her.

Rosemary and Rags;
When Rags was a puppy

School Days - - School Daze

Ash Creek School was a mile south of the Hockenberry house at a country gravel crossroads. It was directly across the road from the home of Walter "Chick" Higgins and his wife, Maude. "Chick" was the head of the school board and he also ran the school -- much to the aggravation of some teachers and parents.

The white school structure, with its bell tower, made an imposing site to travelers on the dusty roads. It was the community meeting hall as well as a one-room school for about 14 children in the surrounding radius of two miles.

Three concrete steps led to the huge front door. Sometimes the door was too heavy for smaller students to handle and the teacher always stood by to manage and patrol the students --unless the door was held open by a big hook on the side of the door-way. The narrow entry was lined with metal coat hooks under a long shelf. This was where we hung our coats and put our overshoes under our assigned hook. A rack in the corner held folding chairs for community activities and held the long hemp rope attached to the bell in the tower. This was a space that was "off limits" to all students.

Two doors at either end of the hall allowed entrance to the main room. This was our classroom. The aroma of chalk dust and pencil shavings, along with the "wet puppy" smell of woolen mittens warming around a big coal stove, are smells that never leave my memory. They were forever present in this huge room, having been absorbed by the wooden desks and the oiled floor. A towering black coal stove stood guard in the back of the room. It was taller than any of us and we were taught to have a great deal of respect for it. It was Hot! A coal bin in the back was closed off from the classroom; but when the teacher opened the door to get another hod of coal, we could feel the bitter winter Kansas wind.

The wooden desks were lined according to sizes and they all faced the front of the room where the chalk boards and the teacher's desk were elevated on a raised platform. A bench was placed in front of the teacher's desk so that each class could come forward and recite the lessons. Thus, it was known as the "recitation bench". The little desks were for the grades one, two, and three; then the bigger ones were for grades four through eight. Each desk had a flat writing surface with a pencil slot, an ink-well, and a shelf under the top to house our books, papers, crayons, and pencils. The desk tops often sported the initials of former students who were probably told, "Do not carve on the desk!" We would all read the engravings and speculate as to whose brother or sister was the culprit. I don't know what the punishment was for branding the desks because I felt that it was a dead giveaway to put your initials on something that was not yours. The teacher wasn't dumb and she could figure out who "RD" was! (Rosemary Dague)

Since there was no electricity, we were grateful for large windows on the north and south sides of the room to provide plenty of light. Coal oil lamps provided light on really dark days or for evening programs. There was no running water; so we went out to the cistern and pumped pails of water for drinking and washing our hands. Near the front door of the classroom were two tables --one for holding a wash basin, soap, and towels; another held a large stone crock for our drinking water. One ladle was used to dip into the cool liquid and fill our individual cups. We were to use only our cup that had our name on it; and we were to take it home weekly for a good washing. Sometimes kids would forget to return their cups and would take a drink directly from the ladle. Perhaps that's why we all seemed to come down with the same type of illnesses. As for toilets, we had two out-houses in the back yard -- one for boys and one for girls. Naturally, the boys often teased the girls around the girls' toilet and we'd have to "tell the teacher".

A pantry to the side of the entry housed the supplies that the teacher would need (chalk, tablets, and a first-aid kit) plus all of our lunch pails. Since there was no refrigeration, this was the coolest place to store our food and it was closed off from the classroom. It was also used for a dressing room when there were accidents, or when we put on Christmas plays. We could usually find Santa hiding out in there to remain out of the little ones' sight. I found it to be a great place to roll down the horrid brown full-length stockings that hooked onto my underwear. Momma insisted that I wear them to keep my legs warm. No other girl had to wear long socks. So to fit in with all the other girls, I'd go into the pantry, roll down my stockings, and be just like them. When the school day ended, I'd re-enter the pantry, roll up my socks, and hook them up again. I thought Momma would never realize that I was doing this. How foolish I was! One afternoon she asked why I never got the knees in my stockings dirty; but I would often have scrapes and scratches on my real knees. I had to confess. My confession, however, didn't stop me. I'd still roll the stockings down; but at the end of the day, I'd get down on my hands and knees and get the stockings soiled. I really should have been praying to God instead of making a laundry problem for Momma. She never confronted me about this again. She probably realized that I was one stubborn little girl.

Our playground was huge. It was on both sides of the school and about 50 yards in back of the school. It was big enough to have a ball diamond where we played softball. There were two swings, a teeter-totter, a slide, and a rickety merry-go-round that was removed during my first year. Beyond the ball diamond there was a farm that had a pond on it. During the winter we were given permission to skate on the pond. I didn't have a pair of skates, and I wouldn't have known how to use them if I had owned a pair; but it was such fun to slide on my galoshes-clad feet. When the spring weather warmed the ice, we'd often hear it cracking. What an eerie sound! That was the time the teacher would yell for us to get off the ice and to stay away from the pond. We were never allowed to go there when the ice had melted and the water would be rippling in the Kansas wind.

Ash Creek, the one room school without all the fancy trimmings that schools now have, was the place that I was so anxious to attend. At this time there was no such thing as kindergarten in the country schools; so the grades were from one through eight. Kansas law stated that a child could enter school at the age of six. Here I was, five years old and wanted desperately to go to school and to have playmates. Would I really have to wait another year? Couldn't I be enrolled at the age of five years and five months? Oh, please, let me give it a try.

Momma pleaded my case with Mr. Higgins and the teacher, Miss Leisher. "Rosemary is really excited about attending school. There are six other children in the neighborhood that will be in the first grade. If we wait until next year, Rosemary will be the only child in her class. Carl and I would really like for her to have the competition of others in the class. Since she's an only child, she really needs to learn to work with others."

Mr. Higgins didn't object and Miss Leisher merely replied, "If Rosemary can keep up with the others in her class, I'll accept her. Five and a half isn't too far away from six." Little did Miss Leisher know that I really liked her for letting me start early. She was not only pretty -- she was nice!

Shopping for school supplies was so exciting. I got a green imitation leather book satchel, a Big Chief wide-lined tablet, a yellow box of Crayola crayons, a 12 inch ruler, some soft-lead pencils, and a big pink eraser. Lunch time at school would mean that I'd have to carry a packed meal. I got a green metal domed lunch-box with a thermos in the top compartment. I imagined that lunch would be like a picnic everyday.

Weeks before school started in September; I'd pack and unpack my satchel. I'd pretend that I was going to school and sit at my desk in the corner of the kitchen and take the role of teacher as well as student. When the Labor Day holiday was over, school began. I was ready! I had picked out what I was going to wear and was eager for Daddy to drive me to school. There were no school buses, so parents either drove their children or bikes were ridden. For the first year Daddy or Momma drove me to school and we'd share rides with the Rogers and Ryland families. Rain or snow, we made the trip. Today I marvel at all of the "snow days" that the children have. Some of our best school days were in the snow -- why stay home? If the teacher could make it to school, so could we.

My first grade class was a big one for a country school. There were seven of us:

                Melee Cutshawl
                Rosemary Dague (that's me!)
                Sharon Haddee
                Melvin Hubbard
                Lyle Rogers
                Carol Rogge
                Ruth Ryland

When our class was called to the recitiation bench, we filled it. The five girls always sat at one end and the boys sat at the other. The boys were afraid they'd get "cooties" from us. If we caused a commotion, Miss Leisher would have us sit alphabetically. I really didn't mind because that meant that Melvin and I would sit nearer to each other. Sometimes Sharon would be absent and that meant that Melvin and I would get to sit side-by-side. Since we liked each other, we'd be attentive.

Everything about school was fine; but lunch was not the picnic that I expected it to be. Momma packed good sandwiches; but I was not one to be excited about peanut butter and jelly, pimento cheese, or bologna every day. It got really boring. I missed breaded pork chops, hot fried chicken, Swiss steak, pot roast, mashed potatoes -- well you can see where I'm headed. I really missed a big home-made dinner. The one thing that I always liked was my thermos of cold Ovaltine or Bosco chocolate milk. The other students were getting bored with their lunches, too; so we decided to trade our food. We would swap a banana for a cupcake, or a chicken leg for a candy bar, or a blue plum for two oatmeal cookies. We thought we were doing this without our moms ever knowing; but when strange candy wrappers or dried chicken bones, or banana peels, or plum pits arrived home in our lunch boxes when they weren't brought from home, our secret was out. Momma wasn't too pleased with the idea of lunch swapping; but what could she do? I think she talked with the other moms and they decided on good choices to pack in our lunches. Two things offered to me for a swap that I would never take were a cold fried egg sandwich or a cup of Cream of Wheat from someone's breakfast. Yuck!

Learning was fun and I soaked it up like a blotter absorbing spilled ink. Reading opened new doors for me and I tried so hard to get it right. English is a funny language, especially for a beginner. The beginning words and sentences in our "Primer" were relatively simple and I breezed through them. However, when it came to other sources like a geography lesson, I was baffled. I argued with Miss Leisher that the word **island** should really be pronounced **"is land"**. She corrected me and I persisted. I was stubborn! At the supper table that evening, I told my parents that Miss Leisher was wrong; she didn't know how to pronounce the word **island**. "She's pretty dumb! Doesn't she know that **is** is **"is"** and **land** is **"land"**, so the word has to be pronounced **"is land"**."

"Rosemary, your teacher is correct in pronouncing the word "island". You need to know that the English language has some weird things about it; but you don't know everything. Let Miss Leisher teach you. You need to be a good student and not always challenge others. As you grow, you'll learn what is correct and what is incorrect. That's when you can raise questions in a polite way. I want you to show Miss Leisher respect." My argument ended suddenly when Momma laid down the law.

I'm sure that Momma was worried that Miss Leisher might be put out with me and decide to set me back to the first grade next year. Momma wanted me to listen and learn and to keep my mouth shut. I did just that when another strange word crept into my reading. The word was **"gn**at**"**. I didn't challenge Miss Leisher this time; but secretly I'd pronounce it **"guh-nat"** just to be devilish. I still do this even now. Crazy words like "knife" and "knock" take me back to my first grade year. But I heeded Momma's advice. I kept my mouth shut and didn't argue.

Miss Leisher, a young, pretty, first-year teacher, had a difficult time with some of the older boys like Doyle Dague and Venon Rogge. Perhaps she had a hard time with a certain little first grader by the name of Rosemary, too! It didn't help that Mr. Higgins from across the road was over many times to give her advice. It made us think that Mr. Higgins didn't have faith in Miss Leisher or her ability to teach. She resigned after one year. I believe that she got married and decided to leave the one-room school.

The teacher for my second and third years was a grandmotherly lady by the name of Mrs. Durst. She was nice; but I remember her as "gray" -- gray hair, gray attitude, and a gray approach to learning. She was strict and able to control the boys; but she didn't have a "fun" personality. Although I did well in my lessons, I felt that everything was too "down-pat" with no variety. We had to memorize a lot of things.

Then at the beginning of my fourth grade, I was about to be rocked to my core when I encountered a wonderful teacher for my grades 4 through 8. His name was Mr. Wayne Wilgers. This young man (probably 20 years old) began his first year of teaching in Ash Creek. He was good-looking, with dark brown hair, brown eyes, and a dazzling Ipana smile. (Don't misunderstand me -- I didn't have a crush on him -- I had a crush on Melvin Hubbard; but Mr. Wilgers was handsome!) My first two teachers were nice; but they lacked the spark of enthusiasm that I was soon to encounter when I met Mr. Wilgers. He was like a Fourth of July celebration -- bright, energetic, and eye-opening! It was somewhat revolutionary that a man would become an elementary teacher and take a job teaching in a country school. It really changed the idea of the "litle ole' school marm" from by-gone days.

One important change in the school was that Mr. Wilgers was <u>in charge.</u> When Mr. Higgins would come over to see how things were running, Mr. Wilgers would politely set him straight. Mr. Wilgers knew how to start the fire in the rotund stove and how to bank the coals at night. He knew how to fill the coal oil lamps and how to use the blue saw-dust-like floor cleaner for the oiled wood floor. Mr. Wilgers also disagreed with Mr. Higgins about ringing the bell every morning. "Everyone knows that class starts at 8:30. Why ring the bell? No need to make all that noise. I have better things to do with my time," Mr. Wilgers adamantly stated. He could not only handle the maintenance; but he could handle Mr. Higgins as well. I believe Mr. Higgins was disappointed that his services and advice were no longer needed.

Rules were set up for all of us to follow and Mr. Wilgers expected good behavior from all of us. The recitation bench was seldom used unless the individual class needed to work on remedial things like reading, spelling, and the multiplication tables; which we all had to learn by heart. Mr. Wilgers thought that since the one room allowed for all conversations to be heard, everyone had an opportunity to contribute to the lesson if they raised their hand and were acknowledged. This gave everyone an opportunity to learn from each other and to assist others; but we all had to listen and pay attention. We could never interrupt a person who was speaking and would be reprimanded if we did. Laughter was allowed when things were humorous -- but we were never allowed to laugh at someone's mistake or miscalculation. There was a sense that, "We're all in this together", so we became a very tight, yet friendly unit.

Mr. Wilgers had a way of teaching that made learning fun. He taught us in such an easy way that we didn't realize that we were learning. For example: He'd read a story that he had created. Before he came to its conclusion, he'd stop and ask us to write an ending for it. The little first and second graders could tell their ideas orally since they couldn't write; but the grades 3-8 were expected to write their ending using proper sentence structure, grammar, spelling, and a proper conclusion to the story that was originally read aloud. This meant that we all had to listen to the story, create our own ending, write it correctly, and then stand before the class and recite our masterpiece. This simple lesson incorporated listening skills, creative thinking, correct English usage and spelling, and the opportunity to speak in front of the class. Some of the stories required serious thought -- others were whimsical and could end in a humorous fashion. It was fun to listen to all the ideas from the other students. Mr. Wilgers would always end the lesson with his own original conclusion that he had omitted in the beginning of the assignment.

He encouraged us to read and to talk about the books that we enjoyed. Our classroom had a small library and Mr. Wilgers checked out books from the Washington County Library to be used in class. He also encouraged us to get a library card. I did, and I met the nicest lady librarian who helped me through the years to select good books. Oh, yes, we had the standard written book reports; but often at lunch break or at recess, Mr. Wilgers would join us and talk about the books we were reading "just for fun". I always loved horse stories. My favorite author was Thomas C. Hinkle who wrote numerous stories about wild horses in the West. Then in the eighth grade, I read Anna Sewall's **Black Beauty**. What a nice practice to talk to kids in an adult manner about their reading. It reminds me of my friends today who like to share their reading selections with me.

We even learned things during recess. We made and flew kites, studied cloud formations, looked for rocks and herbs, and in the winter, built igloos like the Eskimos.

This last project only happened when the snow storms were huge (5-6 inches or more). Remember, we never had "snow days" so that we could stay home; we had Snow Days so that we could play and learn. The first part of this assignment was to bring an extra snow suit, mittens, and boots. We needed to remain warm and dry. Since the side of our play yard was near the graded road, there was a deep "grader ditch" that always filled with the drifted snow. This was our "snow laboratory" where we tunneled in and under the drifts. We were careful to pack the snow down so that it would not collapse. Then we'd get water and sprinkle it on our tunnel so that it would freeze for the next day. Mr. Wilgers would get waxed produce boxes from a grocery and we'd fill them with water from the cistern. Overnight the boxes would freeze and the next day we'd remove the ice blocks and form igloos. When we did this project, our assignments consisted of study about the Polar region and the Eskimos. It was almost like being there.

When we returned inside the classroom, we'd remove our mittens, snowsuits, and boots and put them around the stove to warm and dry for the next day. That's when the "wet puppy" smell of fourteen pairs of wet woolen mittens warming by the fire filled the room. With rosy red cheeks from the cold and noses that continuously ran, we would begin our bookwork again. Sometimes we hated to see the warm weather melt our handiwork; but we'd move on to another project. We could always bet that Mr. Wilgers had something new up his sleeve.

Outside recess was every day unless it was raining; then we'd stay inside and play games. Some of my favorites were jacks and dominoes along with games like "hang man" and "tic-tac-toe". When the weather was nice, we'd play softball if we could get nine players together. The big kids got the prime positions and some of the little ones served as fielders because most of us never hit the ball far enough to make it to the out-field. If we couldn't form a team, Mr. Wilgers would go to bat and hit fly balls to us. I remember that I complained to Daddy that when I'd catch a high fly, my fingers would be bent backward and my knuckles would hurt. That's when I got an old ball glove that Daddy found in the closet. The glove served me well because during the 8th grade, our team played a neighboring school from Linn, Kansas. The score was tied. It was the bottom of the 9th and Linn was at bat. The western sun was hot and brutal. I wasn't the best player and took my usual position in left field. It was hot and I was tired; so I put my gloved hand up to my face to shield my eyes. Then all of a sudden -- Pow! Much to my surprise and elation, a ball landed right in my glove. I won the game without even trying! Of course I never admitted it until now. (Don't tell!)

Not all of my recesses were happy ones. My second cousin, Doyle Dague, liked to tease me. He knew that Melvin and I liked each other and would meet at the Major Theater in town to see a double-feature on Saturday afternoon when our parents were shopping. Doyle would tease and taunt us by saying:

> "First comes love,
> Then comes marriage,
> Then comes Rosemary and Melvin
> Pushing a baby carriage."

Doyle was inquisitive and would ask Melvin, "Have you kissed her yet?" For the record, Melvin had never kissed me. Oh, we did hold hands in the movie, but that was none of Doyle's business. Then Doyle said that he wanted to kiss me. I was emphatic that he was not going to kiss me; after all, he was a distant cousin! Day after day Doyle would tease and chase me around the playground. I should have told Mr. Wilgers about my dilemma, but I didn't. I was stubborn and could fight my own battles -- or so I thought!

One day, as the wild chase was on, I ran near the fence row and found a rotted fence post that was on the ground. I grabbed it in my right hand and swung it back-handed to my right just as Doyle was nearing me from that side. Bam! The post hit him in the upper chest and then shattered into pieces. It took the wind out of Doyle's sails. He fell to the ground, caught his breath, and then started to cry. He was probably more surprised than hurt. Of course this drew everyone's attention -- especially Mr. Wilgers'. I knew that I was going to be in big trouble; but I'd tell the truth and stand up for myself. I didn't mean to hurt Doyle; but I wanted him to leave me alone.

We were taken aside as we told our accounts to Mr. Wilgers and he had words for both of us. "First off, Doyle, you should have left Rosemary alone when she asked you to stop many weeks ago. When someone says "No", that means "No". Then turning to me, he continued: "And you, little lady, don't use violent means to solve your problems. Come to me, the teacher, or someone in authority and it will be handled. I will be having both of your parents at school for a meeting and I will expect to see both of you at that time also."

Inez and Alvery Dague and my parents joined Doyle and me after school the next day for a meeting with Mr. Wilgers. I worried that Doyle's parents would be mad at me; but when Mr. Wilgers explained what had transpired, it was agreed that both Doyle and I had made some bad choices. I realized that I was mistaken by taking action into my own hands -- that's the job of authority figures. It was my first and last time to be sent to the teacher's desk or office for an infraction. I had learned my lesson and so had Doyle. He stopped chasing and teasing me. I guess he figured out that I could be dangerous.

Four years flew by and I was finishing the 8th grade. So much had happened. Along with the academic work, we also had Christmas plays and singing, entries into the Washington County Fair of samples of penmanship and art projects; and in the spring there was always a program to help graduate the 8th graders into high school. When the County Test for Placement into the high school level was scored, we were all proud to learn that Ash Creek ranked number one in the county school category. Thanks to Mr. Wilgers for his fine teaching skills and his projection that learning was important as well as fun, we were able to score so well. He didn't teach the test; he taught the important basics and facts that comprised the test and then let us arrive at the correct answers on our own. I will always remember him as the teacher who inspired me to continually learn, to question, to obey, and to enjoy life around me. Thanks, Mr. Wilgers.

A Home of Our Own

    My home area of northeast Kansas was one of rolling hills, groves of trees, and small plots of pastures and farm land. A typical farm might consist of 80 or 100 acres -- not like the sections of farm land in western Kansas. In fact, the scene has often been compared to that of Hanover, Germany. Such a settlement named "Hanover" was established about 15 miles from my home. Historically this was also the place where the Pony Express crossed into Kansas from St. Joseph, Missouri. Today metal sculptures of Indians, bison, and Pony Express riders on speedy ponies dot the rolling hills to mark the early mail route. What fun it is to see an unexpected form as you travel along Highway 36. It makes the history of this area come alive.

    When people hear that I am originally from Kansas, they immediately roll their eyes and imagine nothing but flat land. From my point of view, the patch-work formation of farms filled with rustic houses, rows of corn, patches of golden wheat, and fenced pastures dotted with herds of cattle are nothing short of breathtakingly beautiful. It presents an emblem of hard, tedious work done by strong men and women who battled the elements of nature. Sometimes the farmers were victorious; other times they were defeated by wind, heat, and drought.

    My Daddy and his parents were some of those victorious farmers. Daddy loved the outdoors and nature. I can't imagine him doing anything other than farm; but when he was a freshman in high school, a banker wanted him to consider that as a career. When Daddy's family moved from Morrowville to Washington, he dropped out of high school and the offer made by the banker was dropped. I'm sure it was the right choice because I can't imagine Daddy in a business suit sitting behind a desk. He always wore Key brand bib-overalls, oiled leather Red Wing lace-up shoes, and a straw hat in summer; and a wool felt hat with ear muffs, plus a heavy wool mackinaw in winter. I always loved the fact that Daddy had a "farmer's tan" -- his face and arms were bronze; but when he removed his hat and gloves, his light skin on his bald head showed where his hat had shaded him and his hands showed the demarcation of where his gloves had been. All farmers had this type of tan -- it was a "badge of farming". You could always spot a farmer amid the pasty-white town's people.

Because we were renting Mrs. Hockenberry's farm, Daddy wanted property of his own to improve and develop. He already had an 80 acre farm, but there were no buildings on that property. Daddy wanted to live in a better house with up-dated features that he knew were going to be available. Mrs. Hockenberry certainly wasn't going to make improvements; and Daddy didn't want to put his own money into rental property.

Mr. and Mrs. Graves lived ½ mile south of us. Upon their deaths, their 80 acres were put up for sale. Daddy made an offer to the daughter, Ardith Graves, and it was accepted. We were all pleased and excited about the upcoming move. Of course there was plenty of work ahead for us. The property had been vacant for some time, and it was in need of repair. However, when it's a "home of your own", you're willing to put dollars and sweat into it. That's just what Daddy and Momma did.

The Graves' house was a one-story frame cottage set back from the road. The gravel dust wouldn't be such a problem as it was in the other house. A chicken house and a barn were behind the main house. Mrs. Graves was a self-taught botanist who enjoyed different varieties of flowers and trees. The lot around the house was densely covered with mosses, lily-of-the-valley, tansy, ivy, and species that we had no idea as to what they were. The many trees shaded the house and a purple wisteria vine completely covered the wooden trellis over an iron gate that led to the cement walkway to the side porch. It seemed like a jungle to me in comparison to the stately two-story Hockenberry house that was void of landscaping. There was one huge tree by the side of the house. One of its branches was large enough to bear the weight for a rope swing. I had never had a tree-swing before, and the idea delighted me. This was one of the first "improvements" that Daddy made. (Do you suppose it was done on purpose to keep me out of mischief while the others worked on the house?) I would spend hours swinging back and forth, trying to go higher and higher; or I'd wind-up the ropes and go whirling around and around like a spinning top. The green canopy of leaves gave me shade on hot summer days; and when I was tired of swinging, I'd sit quietly and read a story or look at **Wee Wisdom** magazine.

Because of all the foliage around the house, it seemed very cool and moist. I suppose this garden scheme was planned in order to keep the house insulated from the Kansas wind and heat. Dark green roller shades at every window made the rooms cool, yet dark and dreary. Some of the shades had rotted and allowed pin dots of sunlight to stream through. They cast eerie beams of light on the dusty floors. All this darkness and a musky scent that permeated the rooms didn't dampen Momma's spirit. She had bright ideas; and best of all, I was to get a room of my own.

As I toured the house for the first time, I was in awe of a big piece of furniture that was left behind by the previous owners. It was taller than I. A deep mahogany brown finish on the wood made it seem very pretty, even in the dusty setting of the vacant house. Momma dusted the lid and lifted it to reveal a turn-table with a grooved recording of "Red Wing" on it, and a phonograph needle was positioned in the arm. "This is an RCA Victrola", Momma informed me. "Look here. I'll turn this handle to wind up the machine, and gently place the arm on the record. Let's listen!"

I had never seen such a big phonograph. Dorothy had a small, portable phonograph that she played in her room or she carried it with her wherever she went. She had a record collection that included The Ink Spots, Harry James, Frank Sinatra, and Spike Jones. I remember a newly created plastic record that had colored pictures embedded in it to show the Spike Jones band in a wild perfomance of "Cocktails for Two". This giant Victrola was new to me and I delighted in the sound of a man's baritone voice when he began to sing: "Oh, the moon shines tonight on pretty Red Wing". I played that recording over and over. The volume was much louder than Dorothy's little portable machine; but you sure couldn't move this big Victrola around very easily.

Momma and Daddy were busy refurbishing the house. First off, a new coat of deep gold paint with white trim turned the drab exterior into a thing of beauty, especially with all the green foliage around it. Since the trees and shrubs had been trimmed, the jungle-like appearance was turned into a park-like setting. The interior walls were prepared for papering. I remember the task of tearing off the old green paper. We steamed it and I'd have fun taking a wide-blade scraper and peeling off the old moist paper. Momma borrowed wallpaper books from the hardware store and we'd pour over them gathering ideas as to what we wanted in the rooms. Momma wanted something bright and alive --

no more dark greens and no more window shades. She liked the idea of crisp white curtains and draperies on the sunny windows to provide shade when we needed it. The decorating fashion of the day was to have big, bold flowers on the wall. That's just what Momma selected. One room had a burgundy background with huge white hibiscus flowers as the pattern. When Momma put the white sheer curtains at the sunny bay window along with her African violets, it was absolutely beautiful. Mrs. Sloop, the paper hanger from town, marveled at how pretty this old house looked. The transformation from something drab to something vibrant was amazing.

I was tickled to get my very own room. I had always slept on a bed in the corner of my parents' room or on the davenport in the living room. Now I was going to have a big room and a big bed. The color that I wanted for my décor was lavender. Momma helped me select a lovely wall paper with a light lavender background with an all-over sheer daisy design of white. The white curtains and a white "hob-nail" design bedspread made my room elegant. Grandma made some purple throw pillows for accent. It was just perfect for my little stuffed Angora cat that I placed on a pillow on my bed. I was beginning to love this house!

All summer we were busy settling in and making the house a home. With fall just around the corner, Daddy thought it was high time to install a new heating system. We still had the old green coal and wood stove that we put in the front room; but Daddy wanted a propane gas stove for the middle room that we used as our dining room and family room. A large silver propane tank was put in the side yard and pipe was run to the house. For the first time in my life, I experienced gas heat in my home. It was so easy to just turn the lever and "pouf" a blue flame would appear to light the ceramic burners and heat would be forth-coming. It provided wonderful warmth for both the middle and front rooms when the weather wasn't too cold. However, when the weather got blustery, we would close off the front room with pocket doors that were between the rooms. No need to heat the entire house. Of course our bedrooms would be cold -- but we took care of that by using lots of blankets, quilts, and flannel pajamas. Often we'd dress, one at a time, near the gas stove in the dining room or by the gas cooking stove in the kitchen.

The new kitchen gas stove was a marvel-- no more wood was needed to heat the stove early in the morning to get ready for breakfast. Again, all you had to do was to turn the knob and "pouf", the burner was ready to go. Momma was thrilled with the new appliance and she cooked wonderful meals on it. She particularly liked the oven for its accurate temperature. Now she could bake angel food and chiffon cakes to perfection.

The holidays were nearing and Daddy had a wonderful idea for a family gift -- a propane gas refrigerator! We still didn't have electricity; but with the installation of the propane gas, we were able to get a Servel refrigerator. I really didn't understand the fact that a pilot light would light a burner and get a chemical going that would chill and freeze the upper section and keep the lower level cool; but the thought of having ice cream whenever we wanted it was out of this world.

I remember the day that the refrigerator was delivered. It was a cold January day-- rather strange to get a refrigerator when we could keep things cold out on the back porch; but we were all excited about "Servy" Servel. (We always named things. "Kenny" was for our Kenmore gas stove and "Magic" for our Magic Chef cooking stove.) With our new appliance we would no longer have to buy a block of ice to put in our ice box. The fact that we could make ice cubes was fun -- even in the winter. Then the best recipe of all came my way -- Kool Aid popsicles in the form of ice cubes on sticks. My favorite flavor was orange. I believe I had an orange mouth all winter. Funny thing though, when summer rolled around, I didn't make the popsicles as often as I once did. The newness had worn off, and I moved on to making chocolate ice-cream sodas and other yummy treats.

A tree-swing, new bicycle, orange popsicles, gas heating and cooking -- could life get any better? I didn't think so. Life was really good at the Graves' house. I was a half mile closer to school so I could ride my new bicycle. I learned to ride my bike in the big yard and the long gravel lane. The concrete walkway was a good starting place. Daddy would follow behind me holding the bike seat steady as I pedaled down the grassy slope of the front yard. I always trusted that he was there to help balance me; but one time I looked back and saw Momma and him smiling and standing by the porch as I had ridden the bike all by myself. Once I had learned to keep my balance, I was able to ride anywhere. Most of my traveling was on our lane to and from the mail box. There wasn't as much gravel there as on the county roads. Gravel roads aren't easy to manage on a bike; but I was able to do well. When a car approached, I would carefully get off my bike and wait by the side of the road in the deep gravel before I'd get on the bike again. I felt very big as I rode to school. My books were in my front basket and I had a horn that made an "Ooga, Ooga" noise when I pushed it.

One day I noticed several big equipment trucks loaded with long creosote poles and posthole diggers driving past our drive. Other trucks carried huge wooden spindles of heavy cable. Sometimes I'd ride my bike to the end of our drive and watch all the trucks pass by. "What're all the big trucks doing on our road, Daddy?" I was not only curious, I was also a little miffed that I couldn't ride on the country road because the trucks were too big and riled up too much dust. Why couldn't they drive down another road?

"Our life is about to get a whole lot better, Rosemary. You see, a government program called REA is coming to Washington County." Daddy could see that the initials meant nothing to me. "REA stands for Rural Electrification Administration and it provides electricity for us here in the country if we sign up for it. I've already signed and we'll be getting electricity soon. Then we'll be just like the city folks!" I could see that Daddy was proud to have this property and to be able to fix it up nicely. Exciting times were ahead.

In the days to come, I'd see many trucks and workers pass by. Now I'd smile and give them a big wave because I wanted them to hurry and dig the holes, put up the poles, and string the cable. I could hardly wait to get lights that turned on by a flick of a wall switch. As we'd drive to and from town, we'd notice the advancement of the REA poles and lines. This made the landscape appear to have tall sentinels marching mile after mile with the magic cable strung between them. They were getting closer and closer. When Daddy was notified that we were the next mile to be hooked up, we had to get an electrician to wire our house. Momma and I went shopping for ceiling light fixtures and light bulbs. There was to be one ceiling fixture in every room -- even the closets! I had remembered seeing light bulbs in the grocery store; but they were never used by us. Now I was proud when we checked out with dozens of bulbs. "Looks like you're getting hooked up with the 'juice'", the store clerk joked. We were indeed!

As each farm was "hooked up", the farmer would keep the yard light on all night. Since the dusk-to-dawn lights weren't developed yet, the lights had to be manually turned on and off. The towering yard light shining in the night was a symbol of the farmer saying, "I got hooked up today!" And he would be very proud. Before we got the lines into our house, we would walk down the lane to the main road to see if our neighbors had lights. The REA was probably the most exciting and liberating act that I can remember in my lifetime. It took the farm out of the darkness and it united us with our "enlightened" city cousins.

Now came the purchases of electric appliances. Momma got an electric skillet that she could use anywhere there was an outlet. Boy, she loved cooking on the screened porch when the weather was hot. We traded our tube radios in for cute electric ones -- one for each room. I remember the white one that I got for my bedroom. Of course we got serious appliances too: a vacuum, iron, toaster, mixer, fans, and power tools; the list was endless. All of these seem so run-of-the-mill now; but they were so special to us then.

Perhaps the most liberating and up-dated appliance was an electric pump for our well. With it, we no longer needed to rely on the Morse-Fairbanks steel windmill to pump our water. Now we had the power and the force to pipe water into the house. This meant that we could now install a sink with water faucets, a bathroom lavatory, a bath tub, and a stool. Daddy dug trenches for the pipes to run to the house. He also had a septic tank installed in the back of the yard for toilet waste. Now we had indoor plumbing -- no more carrying water in from the well, no more wash basins, and no more running to the privy for personal trips. All of this was possible due to the REA.

If you've never carried in wood from a wood pile on a daily basis, or lugged a hod of coal into the house; you can't imagine the freedom that a gas stove provided. There were no more splinters of wood or gray ashes to sweep -- no more stove pipes to keep clean and clear. If you've never filled a coal oil lamp, or trimmed a wick, or replaced fragile mantles on a Coleman gas lamp; then you can't imagine how amazing it was to flip a switch and the room would be entirely drenched in glorious light. If you've never carried pails of water from the outside well for drinking and washing; then you can't imagine the thrill of going to a sink and turning the faucets on for water -- both hot and cold. With the additon of a hot water heater, it was possible to take a luxurious bath; no more heating water and getting out the wash tub in order to bathe. It also made laundry day so much easier. Of course you can imagine what an "out-house" was all about -- but with indoor facilities, we were truly living the good life.

So many things changed in our lives with the advancement of REA. Even my one room school was involved with new lighting and water to the classroom; however, the outdoor toilets remained. In the years to come more appliances would be added for the comfort of farm families. Air-conditioning, television, microwave ovens, milking machines, power tools, and computers would provide remarkable comfort for the farm families.

I will always remember the first time we turned on our electric lights in our home. Things would never be the same. I was so proud that Daddy and Momma were willing and able to make changes and to move to a home that they could improve. Had we stayed in the Hockenberry house, we would not have had these amenities because Mrs. Hockenberry didn't want to enroll in the REA. Change is hard; but change is inevitable. I was so thankful that my parents weren't afraid to take the chance and create a good home with the new technology that was available. They were brave. I like to think that I gained the courage to take chances and accept changes from them.

My growing years were spent in this comfortable home. I was six when we moved in and I was seventeen when I left for college. Many changes were made through the years.

New updates like paint, wall paper, and carpets kept the home looking crisp and clean. I learned so much there as I left my childhood days and developed into a young woman. I learned to cook and preserve home-grown produce. Raising chickens, pigs, and cattle gave me an insight into the business of livestock rearing. Watching crops grow into a future profitable harvest gave me an understanding of financial ups and downs. I saw my father hold back tears when a hail storm ruined the wheat crop just days before it was to be harvested. I watched my mother as she balanced the books and ear-marked money for certain needs. I always remember Momma saying, "You can throw more out the back door than your husband can bring in the front." That's where I got my "thrifty" ways.

I also learned about dating and romance here. John Wieland was one of my favorite suitors with a glib sense of humor. One time when I was wearing the fragrance "Wood Hue" by Faberge, he asked what the scent was. "Wood Hue", I replied.

"I sure would!" he smiled with a twinkle in his eye.

Other boys drove out to the farm to take this little farm girl out on dates and proms. They were all good guys and we had many happy times here.

When I entered college at Kansas State, I left this house, never to return to living there on a full-time basis. As much as I love the farm, I did not desire to create a life for myself on it. It takes a special type of person to endure the ups and downs of farming. Patience and faith are traits that every farmer must have in abundance. I felt that I was lacking in both of those. In later years, the house welcomed me back on summer breaks and holidays; just as it welcomed Roy and Ginny and Dorothy and John, and later Bill and our children. Momma and Daddy lived there for many years until health issues forced them to sell and enter nursing homes.

In 2008 I returned to Washington County. The house and out-buildings were no longer standing. The lane and the grove of trees were tilled over and lush crops of corn and milo filled the area. Was this demise of my childhood farm also the result of REA? Perhaps it was. The modernization of the small family farm provided a way for the land owner to accomplish more. The more farm land cultivated, the more profits the farmer could make. I recalled Daddy wanting more land and a better house for his family; so how could I find fault with the new owner of this land who demolished my childhood home? It was his to do with as he desired.

I stopped the car by the side of the graded gravel road. I faced the new landscape, closed my eyes and envisioned the iron gate, the wisteria trellis, the walk to the side porch, and the waft of freshly baked cinnamon rolls coming from the kitchen. Hot tears welled up under my closed eye-lids as I imagined Momma in her apron and Daddy in bib over-alls coming out to embrace me as they had always done. Once again I was a child. Once again, **I was home!**

The Haunting Question

I can't recall why Roy was relocated to Denver, Colorado. Perhaps he was finishing out his Army obligation as a medical technologist in the Fitzimmons Army Hospital. It had been a long time since we had seen him; and Momma, Dorothy, and I decided to make a bus trip to Denver. Dorothy was working in Wichita; but she was able to get a few days off during Easter time.

The Trailways Bus Depot was located in the Washingon Hotel in town. Daddy drove us to the depot early in the morning. He was staying home to keep the farm running. He had a second cousin in Denver who was an administrator of an orphanage. We were invited to stay at her apartment while we were there. She was very happy to learn of our visit and she made plans to show us the city of Denver and the orphanage where she worked.

I was really looking forward to this trip. Seeing Roy again would be so nice; traveling on a bus for the first time would be exciting. I was also going to wear my new coat that had a matching hat. Momma had made it for me from material that Dorothy bought in Wichita. There was nothing that nice in Washington and I was very proud of my new outfit and Momma's great sewing skills. I was a very proud seven year old.

The huge red and beige Trailways bus arrived from Marysville right on time. We all kissed Daddy "Goodbye" while the driver loaded our luggage. The steps were pretty steep for my skinny legs; but I made it up. I was surprised to see a long aisle with two rows of seats on either side. Men and women, both young and old, were staring at us as we boarded. Some gave us a smile; others just studied us as we chose our seats. We were lucky to get three seats close to each other. Momma and I sat together while Dorothy had a seat across the aisle from us. With a "swish" the bus door closed. I gave one last wave to Daddy and then the driver steered the huge vehicle out of the parking space and we were on our way.

I asked Momma if I could get the window seat. She agreed because she wanted to visit with Dorothy. What a good view of the city I had as we drove down Main Street. I waved at a few people whom I recognized. I felt very "big" being a traveler. The route to Denver would be straight out on Highway 36. I saw familiar farms as we drove west of Washington. We crossed the Mill Creek Bridge and I saw the home of Sally Geistfeldt whom I had met during my piano lesson classes. Oh, how I wished that Sally was playing outside while we drove by. I'd wave a big wave to her to let her know that I was on board; but it was too early for Sally to be out playing. Besides, she saw buses and cars travel past her home so often that she probably didn't ever give them a second thought.

The landscape was new to me after we passed Sally's home. We were on our way to Belleville. I noticed warning signs about the winds that blew strong in this area. Reports had been made that huge semi-trucks had been blown off the road and serious injuries had occurred. Kansas is a very windy state and for anyone not realizing the force of the winds as they sweep through the low hills could be taken unaware. I noticed the swaying of the bus as we were buffeted by the currents. One woman in the seat ahead of us said that she felt like she was going to be sick. I really hoped that she'd get her stomach settled, as the idea of smelling puke all the way to Denver was upsetting to my stomach. Thank goodness someone gave her a mint and she said she felt better.

I didn't realize that Denver was so far away. "When will we get there, Momma?" Momma was very patient with me and told me that when the sun went down, we'd be in Denver. My, that would be hours and hours! I was to learn that we would have many stops before we reached our destination. The first stop was Belleville. We couldn't get off the bus because it was a "pick-up" or "drop-off" spot. We had to wait for some passengers to get on board. Just like the people who stared at us when we boarded, now it was our turn to look at them. Some passengers were dressed nicely like we were --dressy clothes and nice shoes. Others simply wore bib-overalls, jeans, or house dresses. Momma always thought that when you left home, you should wear your nice clothes. Maybe those were their nice clothes.

After our first stop, there was Smith Center and miles onward, Phillipsburg where we were to have our lunch and restroom break. Boy, I was ready for both! We had 30 minutes before we were to be back on the bus. The café was a bustle of activity. Everyone placed their orders and hoped that there would be enough time to eat. Momma advised Dorothy and me to get a sandwich, chips, and a drink that we could take back on the bus; just in case we couldn't eat it all there in the restaurant. Some passengers ordered plate-lunch specials like chicken or roast beef. They should have listened to my Momma because when the "On Board" call came from the driver, they weren't finished with their meals.

I felt like an old pro when I entered the bus for the second time and I remembered just where our seats were. I finished the rest of my lunch on board the bus as we started out on the road again, I snuggled down in the maroon velour seat. The swaying of the bus put me to sleep.

When I felt the bus turn and the sound of the brakes making a "poosh" sound, I awakened. "Are we in Denver, Momma?" How disappointed I was to learn that this was just another stop to allow more passengers to board. This time we were in Oberlin --still in Kansas. I was getting fidgety and anxious to get off the bus; but we had many stops to make. By now we had a bus-load of people. When we entered Colorado, I expected to see mountains right away; but the land remained flat, just like Kansas. After many stops at little towns, we finally neared Denver and I could see the Rocky Mountains in the distance. They were some really big hills. I was impressed. The sun was sinking in the western sky and I knew that we would be seeing Roy soon.

The city of Denver was full of lights. It was the biggest city that I had ever seen and I was wide awake with anxious expectations. It was a slow course before we reached the depot; and then we had a slow departure from the bus. "Hurry up, people." I felt like saying, but I didn't. Momma told me to be sure to gather all of my things like the **Wee Wisdom** magazine, crayons, and papers. "Be sure to get your hat", Momma reminded me. I had folded it and put it in the overhead compartment with my coat. "If you leave anything on the bus, it will probably be lost; so remember what you brought with you and be sure to carry it off." That was a good lesson to learn.

Roy was all smiles as he greeted us. He gave us big hugs and lots of kisses. I thought he was more handsome than ever and he thought that I was really pretty in my new coat and hat. We had a nice supper and visit before Roy drove us to the apartment of Daddy's cousin.

Vivian Hyland was a plain-looking lady with dark hair braided and then zigzagged in the back to form a bun. We had never met her before; so we relaxed and got acquainted. Momma had brought pictures to show her. There were lots of pictures of Daddy or "Carl" as Vivian referred to him and pictures of our house.

The apartment was very neat and clean. We were shown to our room and to the bath room. I recall the wonderful Avon soaps that Vivian had. She invited me to use any one that I wanted. I chose "Roses, Roses". Vivian sold Avon, so she had many wonderful samples. As I bathed in the big porcelain tub that night, I delighted in the lather and fragrance of roses. I slept well that night. The long bus ride had really tired me.

The next morning we set out to see Denver. Roy took us to the Fitzsimmons Army Hospital. It was a massive building and it's all a blur to me now. Then we went to the state capitol building. Somewhere along the way, we stopped at a gift shop. I loved to shop and Momma bought me a silver and turquoise ring. It was a little too big for my ring finger, so I wore it on the middle finger of my left hand. "Let's get a photo of the three of you in front of the capitol." Roy aimed the camera at the same time that an annoying itch occurred to me in a very "private" part. As I itched, I also held up my left hand with my middle finger extended to show off my ring. That turned out to be the most embarrassing photo that I have ever taken. I always got kidded about it. At the time, I was innocent of the fact that the middle finger represented a vulgar word. I also learned that when an itch occurs, you don't necessarily have to take immediate action to scratch it!

Vivian wanted to give us a tour of the orphanage. The large brick building with black wrought-iron fencing was as neat and clean as Vivian herself. We went to her office and met some of her co-workers. Then we went out to the courtyard where hundreds of girls my age came running to "Miss Vivian". I know there weren't hundreds, but it seemed like it to me. In the crisp mountain air, I was startled to hear questions that I never expected. "Are you coming to live here?" "When are you moving in?" "Can I be your friend?"

I stood close to Momma. I wanted her to hold me and take me away from these girls. I wondered, "Am I being put in this orphanage? Was this trip only a ploy to put me in this home? Why hadn't I been told?" I felt sick and I didn't want to look at any of the inquisitive girls. For the first time in my life, I felt that I might have to be separated from Momma and Daddy. That was unthinkable and I kept my eyes focused downward as I held back tears.

"No, no, Rosemary isn't coming to live here. We're only visiting Miss Vivian," Momma answered as she put her arm around my shoulder. "We live in Kansas on a farm; and Rosemary has to get back to school." I think Momma must have felt my uneasiness; and those were the most wonderful words that I had ever heard in my life.

Our brief visit was over too soon. We had to say good-bye to Roy and to our hostess, Vivian. We bid farewell to the mountains and to Denver. The long ride home began in the late afternoon; so we traveled in darkness most of the way. I made the mistake of drinking a 12 oz. Pepsi when we had a snack at the depot. Oh, how I regretted it! The rest stop at Phillipsburg was miles away, and I needeed a restroom badly. This was before buses had toilets on them. It was another lesson to learn the hard way. Don't drink too much before starting out on a road trip.

In my misery, it gave me time to think. That question, "Are you going to live here?" asked by one of the orphans, haunted me. I had never known of an orphanage before. What circumstances caused these girls to be placed there? As I looked out the bus window into the darkness of night, I wondered what would happen to those girls. Would they find happy homes like mine? I wondered, too, how I could have ever doubted my mother's love or her intentions for me. I felt guilty for even thinking such a thought. I looked over at Momma and smiled.

The Phillipsburg rest stop finally came and I was one of the first off the bus. What a relief! This time I didn't have any snack or drink during the break. No need to be miserable again. Since this was the destination point for several passengers, the back seat was now available when we re-boarded. Momma and I went back there so that I could sprawl out and get some sleep. She folded her sweater to make a pillow for me and I snuggled into my wool coat. With my bladder, as well as my mind at ease, I fell asleep immediately. Hours later I heard the words, "Next stop, Washington." I immediately awakened, anxious to see Daddy again. Deep down inside, I was so thankful to be home.

Throughout the years, I never mentioned my foolish doubts and fears to Momma. Did she harbor a secret too? Did Momma ever wonder how it would have been to put a child in an orphanage? When she was widowed at a young age, there could have been that possibility of putting her children in a home if she hadn't had the assistance of Aunt Mabel and Uncle Allie (relatives of Momma's first husband). They were able to provide care for Roy and Dorothy when Momma had to work on a nursing case.

We never discussed the episode at the orphanage; yet whenever I recalled this memory, it made me thankful for such a wonderful home where I felt safe, secure, and loved. Momma probably felt thankful too, that she didn't have to be separated from her children. As the character, Dorothy, in **The Wizard of Oz** says, "There's no place like home. There's no place like home." I was so happy to have one.

Momma, Dorothy and me in Denver, Colorado

The Kansas Winds

Summer in Kansas means hot and windy days. These two elements help the wheat to create "amber waves of grain." I recall a day in early June when the winds blew clouds from the southwest. Daddy had gone to town to get some parts for the Allis-Chalmers combine before harvest began in a few weeks. I think all farmers get anxious for the wheat harvest to begin and to be completed before any chance of wind and hail can destroy the crop. Even today, farming is a big gamble -- a beautiful field of golden grain can be destroyed in an instant by the forces of nature.

When Daddy returned with new belts and bolts for the combine; he also had a brown sack with an IGA label on it. Now they didn't sell combine parts at the grocery store; but they did sell ice cream. That's exactly what Daddy had bought -- three pints of Sealtest ice cream.

"Hey, gals, let's sit on the front porch and watch the clouds go by." With that invitation, Daddy headed to the big front porch with a panoramic view of the cloud formations in the west.

Momma liked chocolate, I preferred strawberry, and Daddy had Neapolitan (three level rows of strawberry, vanilla, and chocolate). Small wooden paddles were provided by the grocery store. We ate right out of the little rectangular boxes, so we didn't dirty any dishes or spoons -- what a nice treat on a hot summer afternoon. Even Jiggs, our Boston bull terrier, who usually lounged around inside the house, decided to join us. He knew he'd get to lick the cartons if he'd show up and be patient.

As we were enjoying the treat, the wind began to strengthen. The angry dark clouds from the southwest were beginning to boil and move across the gray sky. I noticed little dirt devils dancing in the gravel driveway. An ominous feeling came over me. Daddy and Momma must have felt the same way too, as their cheerful banter stopped and their eyes focused on the clouds. As the wind swirled around the porch, it blew napkins off our laps; and little Jiggs had a hard time licking the remains of Daddy's Neapolitan box as it scooted across the porch floor. We knew that a storm was headed in our direction.

Then Daddy yelled out, "Look at that!" A dark gray funnel-shaped cloud came swirling out of the threatening clouds. It reminded me of a circus elephant's trunk when the animal is searching the ground for peanuts. This rotating gray "trunk" was rotating around sucking up dust and debris at its base. I was scared. I felt sick. The strawberry ice cream had been refreshing; but now it churned around in my uneasy stomach -- kinda like the storm that was raging across the sky about a half mile away.

"Hurry, let's get the dog and go down to "the creek", Daddy ordered. "The cave will be the safest place for us and we will drive away from the storm." We were headed for Grandpa's farm that was located east of us on the banks of Ash Creek. We left napkins and ice cream boxes on the porch and hurriedly piled into the car; Daddy, Momma, Jiggs, and me. As we took the back road east through the pasture to Grandpa's, I looked over my shoulder to our house. We had done so much work on it and it was so beautiful. Would it still be standing after the storm? Sometimes tornadoes take unusual turns. What appeared to be headed straight for you might be changed by upper wind currents or the lay of the land, like a ravine or creek bed. I hoped that the huge "elephant trunk" cloud would not sweep away our home. With each bump in the road, I held tightly onto Jiggs and said a prayer: "Please, God, keep us safe, and don't let me get sick!"

The wind was picking up speed. Trees in the hedgerow that bordered the pasture were bending over with the force of the wind. Dust was blowing all around us. Then random rain drops bombarded the dusty windshield, making a mud-like concoction. Thank goodness we were nearing Grandpa's farm. As we entered the driveway, Daddy tooted the horn to get his parents' attention. The minute we stopped the car in front of the house, Daddy yelled, "Get to the cave! Mom, Dad, get in the cave right now!"

When we exited the car, Daddy's straw hat blew off his head; but he paid no attention. We were all headed for shelter -- Grandpa, Grandma, Momma, Daddy, and me with little Jiggs still in my arms. We struggled to reach the cave. The wind and the sharp pelting rain drops made the steps very labored.

The cave was near the back door of the house. It was carved out of a hillside. Because of the strong wind force, Grandpa's arthritic hands were unable to budge the heavy oak door. Daddy's strength was able to overcome the winds as well as the weight of the door; and we all desperately entered the safety of the dank chamber. When the door closed behind us, it blocked out the sound of the wind and rain. It also blocked out the light. Grandpa had a big battery-operated lantern for times like this. There were also some smaller flahslights as well as blankets on the table near the entrance. Kansans had to be prepared for tornadoes -- after all, we didn't live in the Land of Oz!

We huddled on benches near the back of the cave. That was where Grandma kept all of her canned goods. Mason jars were filled with home-grown produce: green beans, corn, tomatoes, carrots, cherries, and assorted jams and jellies topped with white paraffin. Those jars were testimonies to the hard work that Grandpa and Grandma did on the farm. There was a layer of dust on the jars, so it was difficult to discern what was in each one. Grandma knew just where each item was located, however, so she knew where to go to get a particular kind of food. I dusted some jars while Jiggs smelled the new territory. The musty cave smell was unfamiliar to him. Besides, we had to do something to keep the storm off of our minds.

After approximately ten minutes, although it seemed like hours, Daddy went to the cave door and listened for any sound of wind. He gingerly opened it and peered out. We all wondered what he would see. Would it be wreckage or would it be normalcy? We were fearful and apprehensive. My ice cream was beginning to churn around again in my tummy. I wished I hadn't eaten so much.

Jiggs followed Daddy and poked his nose out the open door. Soon he slid through the opening and was outside. He had to use the bathroom, so he was in a hurry. When Daddy fully opened the door, we all surveyed the area. The smell of fresh rain was a welcomed fragrance from the stale cave air. All was well. The heavy green metal chairs and the wooden rockers were blown across the lawn. Flowers were bent over as if they were shielding their bodies from the assailing wind. They had survived and would raise their heads again. Like the flowers, we raised our heads and walked out of the dank cave with faces looking upward to the sun. How quickly things can change. One minute its calm and I was eating ice cream and rocking back-and-forth on the front porch; then the furious storm lashed out at us and we ran for safety. When the storm passed, we were back to normal, at least here on Grandpa's place; but what about our home two miles west? I knew that was a worry in the minds of Daddy and Momma.

After setting the chairs upright on the veranda, Daddy went to the car and anxiously said, "Let's get on back to our place, Clara. Sure hope it's OK. Hope the house and the cattle are safe; hope the wheat hasn't been trampled down by the wind; but thank God we're all right." With that he gave a wave to his parents, whistled for Jiggs to jump in the back seat, and Momma and I got in the car. We traveled with a lot of "hope" in our hearts.

This time the trip was less bumpy. Daddy drove much slower over the pasture road for two reasons. He had to drive through mud and water in the ruts of the dirt path. Then he wanted to see the cattle. "I hope they didn't huddle around the hedge trees. There are so many branches down." Daddy studied the pasture with questioning eyes. "Oh, there they are!" A sigh of relief could be heard in his voice. He pointed to the herd. They had clustered at the base of an eastern slope of a small rolling hill away from the tornado damage. Daddy stopped the car and got out in the mud to whistle to his herd -- his bovine buddies. They all looked up and started toward us as they heard the familiar call of their master. Daddy knew the exact number of cows, calves, and steers that he owned. As they eagerly approached, he counted them all; and they were all present! "Come on buddies; let's get up to the corral for some treats." Daddy came back to the car with a smile on his face. As we proceeded back up the road, we looked for damages as the herd followed us. I could see that these Black Angus cattle were as glad as we to have the storm over and to have survived.

The end of the pasture road took us up past the barn and corral. Some hay bales had been blown around and a few salt blocks were tipped over. Our windmill was still in tact and our pretty little house was in good shape. The white trellis holding the purple wisteria was toppled over; but that could be easily repaired. The hen house and pens were in good condition. Momma noticed that all the chickens were inside the chicken house. They had gone in on their own to get away from the raging winds. With the darkening storm sky, they probably thought that it was nighttime and time for bed. We didn't realize that chickens were that smart.

It was so good to be home. My stomach finally felt better. We had not closed the windows when we made our escape, so there were papers and magazines blown around. We also had some rain spots to wipe away, and some curtains were wet and tangled together. Our home had escaped damage. We were so thankful; but what about our neighbors to the west?

After relaxing for a few minutes and having a Pepsi, Daddy got up and said,"Let's see how the wheat is up on the 80 and see about our neighbors." He had tried to use the crank phone, but couldn't get the Operator. That meant that lines had probably been blown down. Momma combed her hair and got her diamond ring from her dresser. She had left it behind when we went to the cave. Momma always wore her ring when she went somewhere and I imagine she was very worried to have left it behind. She never left it, except for today. The ring, a white gold domed filigree band with a diamond solitaire from her first husband and two smaller diamonds from her Aunt

Rose, was a cherished memory of her first marriage and her youth. (When Momma died, I got the two diamonds from Aunt Rose and had them made into a ring for Suzanne. Upon Suzanne's death, I took her ring and presently wear it on my pinky finger. Now it's one of my cherished memories.)

I clipped the leash onto Jiggs' collar and joined Daddy and Momma in the car. Now the sky was a clear blue and the sun was warming the world. "The western sky was entirely different from an hour ago. One of Momma's favorite religious expressions was "This too shall pass." Well, the verse was right; the horrible storm had passed. As we drove along the gravel county road, we noticed telephone poles down or leaning at a 45 degree angle. No wonder we couldn't use the phone. We were curious about what damage we would see. Even Jiggs was looking out the back window with me. He was so glad to be going along. When we neared the 80, we saw the golden shafts of wheat twisted and blown down to the ground. The concern on Daddy's face was evident. Perhaps the sun would revive the wheat as it would the flowers; or the stalks might have been so bent that the heavy beards of wheat might weigh them down and impede the recovery. Time would tell. "If there's to be a loss, it's better to have it here and not with the loss of any of us." Daddy's words brought home the importance of the <u>living</u> and not the <u>things</u> that crowd our lives.

As we continued to drive, we passed by the houses of our neighbors. So far the damage was minimal. The old Hockenberry house was still standing -- even the rickety back porch. Daddy jokingly said that all the tacks that I had hammered in probably made it too heavy for the wind to sweep it away. We saw Eric and Gladys Rogers picking up a few shingles that had blown off their roof. The Gauby's were straightening blown-over chairs, and Ed and Mabel Nemitz were out picking up broken tree branches. Our waves indicated that we were OK and we were glad to see that they had sheltered the storm. Ash Creek school house, with its white bell tower, was standing tall as we rounded the corner and headed west. As we proceeded westward, we began to notice many changes. More phone poles were toppled; more roofs and out-buildings showed damage; more of the wheat fields had matted stalks. We were getting into an area where the tornado had done some major destruction.

We turned to the north and what had once been a beautiful tree-lined lane was a mish-mash of broken and tangled poplar trees. Daddy had to get out of the car to clear the broken limbs from the road. The stately McNitt home was now a shambles with its southwest side slashed open. The gapping wound revealed the rafters, plaster ripped from the plaster boards, torn and soaked wall paper, shredded and tangled draperies, furniture that was scattered all about, and pictures turned in a topsy-turvy way. The McNitts were known as a well-to-do family with one of the nicest houses in the county. I had been to a club meeting there with Momma once and felt that I was in a palace. I had noticed the pretty mirrors and pictures, the ornate Victorian furniture, deep pile carpets, beautiful crystal and china, and sterling silver flatware. I wasn't used to all those elaborate things; but I admired their beauty. The McNitt's children were grown, so they didn't have to contend with childhood mishaps. They could enjoy the elegance of their stately home. The fierce tornado put a temporary halt to that.

Daddy stopped the car and we immediately got out to give the McNitts our condolences. They were in a state of shock; but they were unhurt. Momma gave Mrs. McNitt a hug. "Carl and I are so sorry. We're here to help salvage some things before nightfall comes." Other neighbors were joining us. Everyone was curious as well as compassionate. That tornado could have taken out any of our houses -- why the McNitt's? Only God knew the answer; but as neighbors, we stuck together and helped each other to overcome tragedies such as this.

I was awed by all the debris scattered around the yard -- photos, books, china, and silverware. It was as if a big table drawer had been overturned and all the contents had been strewn about the yard. The tornado did just that to this house. As we walked about the lawn, we picked up photo albums, papers, pictures, kitchen items, and objects that I had no idea what they were., Daddy warned me about broken glass, so I walked carefully holding Jiggs. I helped the neighbor ladies sort items on the cement steps that had once led to the front door.

As I was busy sorting things, I heard Daddy raise his voice to some strangers who had come upon the scene. "I saw you put that silverware in your pocket. Put it up on the porch where the ladies are putting things in boxes."

"Hey, fella, I found it. I'll keep it!" snarled the stranger. He was a seedy looking character wearing bib-overalls about two sizes too big. He was joined by a woman who had greasy dishwater blonde hair and was dressed in a big over-sized house coat with big pockets. I had never seen these people before. They weren't our neighbors.

When the others heard Daddy's accusation that they were pocketing the sterling silver flatware, they gathered around the unfamiliar couple. Lester and Lee Gauby were strapping fellows and when they joined the commotion, the two interlopers became withdrawn. They couldn't make a get-away because they were surrounded by the local residents.

"How about empting your pockets, both of you, and put the stolen things on the porch." Lester's voice had a sense of authority to it and his size re-enforced his demand. They unloaded lots of silverware, an alabaster clock, and a cut-glass candy dish. No wonder they wore big clothes with lots of pockets. "You're a couple of theives -- a pair of "Looky-Lou's" -- looters who prey on other people's hard luck. You're not welcome here in this neck-of-the-woods. I'm writing down the truck license plate and giving it to the sheriff in town. Maybe you stole the truck, I don't know, but we've all seen your pretty faces and we'll remember you. Now get the heck out of here, and don't come back!"

Everyone cheered Lester, and several remarks in agreement were uttered. Daddy and Lester escorted the two intruders back to their truck and saw them on their way. Alvery Dague said that he'd follow them to get them out of the tornado area. "No need for another family meeting up with these scoundrels. If they go to Linn, I'll follow them; if they go to Washington, then I'll be on their tail. I'll even stop at the jail and report them to the sheriff." With that, the crowd applauded and cheered.

It had been a long day and I was tired. It was nearing supper time and the day would be coming to an end. I abandoned my post on the steps and returned with Jiggs to the car. I plopped down on the back seat; Jiggs stayed outside near the open back door. He was on a leash and I had one end looped around my wrist. If he started to roam, I'd feel the tugging. Momma saw that I was fatigued. She convinced Daddy to drive back home. We had done a lot of "pick-up" work and Daddy would definitely be returning to the site in the morning. The McNitts planned to stay the night there on the farm, as a back shed with cots had been spared. Momma offered them a place to stay; but they wanted to be on their property to protect what was left. I imagine the episode with the looters was fresh in their minds. I had napped a little and was still very groggy. I hadn't noticed that the leash loop was no longer around my wrist. I thought that Momma and Daddy would take care of Jiggs and the closing of the back car doors. Soon we were on our way.

It was slow driving through the rubble and the broken trees; but once we were on the gravel road, Daddy picked up speed. With the bouncing around, I woke up and looked for Jiggs. He wasn't in the back seat with me! Where was he?

"Daddy, Momma! Is Jiggs up there with you? He's not back here. Where is he? Where is he?" My throat was hot inside as I held back my screams. Tears started flowing down my cheeks. I was to have been in charge of Jiggs. Why hadn't I looked after him?

Daddy immediately stopped the car by the side of the road. It was then that I noticed that the leash holding Jiggs was leading to the outside of the car. "Daddy, the back door was closed on the leash. Jiggs has been outside all this time. He's outside!"

"Don't open your door, Rosemary. Don't get out." Daddy's tone of voice told me that he was worried that he'd find Jiggs' body under the back wheel well. My poor little dog! Would he be all right?

Daddy gingerly opened his door, looked down, and then got out of the car. He bent down and picked up an empty leash -- no Jiggs. The "D" ring on the collar had opened, releasing the leash and the name tag when the weight of Jiggs had been forced on it as we picked up speed. By some miracle, Jiggs had been set free; yet his fate was uncertain, as he was a house dog and unaccustomed to being alone in the farm fields.

We turned around in the middle of the road and drove slowly back to the McNitt property. All the while I was yelling out the open window, "Here, Jiggs! Here, Jiggs" Our eyes were searching for him -- a little black and white Boston Bull dog -- yet in all the debris, what looked like a little dog might turn out to be a torn pillow or wads of newspapers in the field. Perhaps Jiggs was injured and he would not be able to run. Perhaps he was dead. My heart felt as if a tornado had torn through it and damaged it like the McNitt house. The tornado caused all of this; but I couldn't blame the tornado for everything. I had been slack in looking after my dog; so I had to accept some of the blame.

When we re-joined our neighbors, they were surprised to see us. "We've lost our little dog, Jiggs," Daddy told everyone. "He was outside the car and when I closed the door, he was on a leash on the outside while we were on the inside. Thank goodness the "D" ring opened and allowed him to be set free; but now we can't find him. I hope you all can keep an eye out for him. Rosemary is heartbroken. If you find him, no matter what his condition, I'd appreciate it if you'd let us know." Everyone showed remorse and vowed that they would keep an eye out for him.

We slowly made our way back home. Nighttime was approaching and it was difficult to spot things in the fields. Down the lane we stopped a friend and asked if he had seen Jiggs. The only time he saw Jiggs was when he noticed us earlier with the dog outside the car; but he thought we were letting him walk. We were going very slowly, so he didn't give it any serious concern. He was very sorry now that he hadn't said something. "Hope you find the little fella." He tapped the back fender as a form of "love pat" to us. Here was that word "Hope" again. I had heard it a lot today; and that was all I had to go on -- HOPE !

The house seemed so empty without little Jiggs bouncing around. Momma was gathering papers and pens to make "LOST DOG" posters. She also created an ad to run in the **Washington County News**. "We'll find him, Rosemary. We'll keep looking." She hugged me and wiped away my tears.

She was such a good mother. Why wasn't I a good mother to Jiggs? I felt guilty.

I wasn't hungry for supper. In fact, none of us ate very much. When it was bedtime, I missed the chore of taking Jiggs out for his bathroom business. The leash was hanging by the door; but the little owner of it was missing. The evening sky was very dark. No moon or stars could be seen. There would be no light for my little dog -- just cold darkness.

It was difficult for me to get to sleep. Momma sat on the side of the bed. We prayed to God for the safety of little Jiggs; and we also gave thanks for our safety from the storm. It had been a topsy-turvy day. There had been good things (ice cream) and bad things (tornado), then good things (our safety) and bad things (destruction at McNitts') followed by a horrible thing. I drifted off to sleep only to be awakend by crackling lightening and rumbling thunder. It was early in the morning and I wondered how Jiggs would survive the storm; or would he survive? I had to keep the positive thought that Momma had told me: "We'll find him, Rosemary." I also thought: "This too shall pass."

In the days that followed, my life seemed like an empty shell. My little playmate was gone. There would be no more dressing him in doll clothes and putting him a doll carriage. He would lie for hours dressed like a baby until a cat crossed the path. Then he'd jump from the carriage in the doll clothes and chase after the cat. It was a funny sight to see him dressed like a baby in a dress and bonnet pursuing the old tom cat!

Every time I passed by his water bowl, his bed, or his toys; my heart ached. Where was he? Why hadn't we gotten any calls from the posters that we had placed in town and on the fence posts? The weekly newspaper was delivered on Thursday and I had hoped that the "Lost" ad would bring in phone calls. It had been a week. I tried so hard to be brave and to have hope. I realized that many of my neighbors had suffered from the tornado damage; but I was suffering too.

Then we began getting phone calls about our missing pet. "Think I have your dog. She seems like a real nice pet. I'll bring her by if you tell me where you live." Well, that dog couldn't be Jiggs. Jiggs was a male! Couldn't they read the ad? Other calls came in and the descriptions didn't fit. Why were people so cruel to get our hopes up and then describe an animal that couldn't possibly fit the description that was mentioned in the newspaper ad? They only wanted to reap the $25 reward. That was a high price in the 1940's.

The days wore on and on. Another week passed. The phone calls became fewer and fewer even though Momma continued to place ads in the paper. Every Saturday was market day in Washington and everyone went to town.

We met our neighbors who asked about Jiggs. They were saddened to learn that he was still lost. Finding him was beginning to seem hopeless to me.

On market day, all the ladies either sat in private autos and visited, or they spent the day shopping. The men gathered around the bank corner talking politics and harvest results while they waited for their wives to finish shopping or gossiping. It was there on the bank corner that Daddy met an old acquaintance from Greenleaf, a town about 15 miles from Washington. "Carl, I overheard you say that the little dog that your daughter lost after the tornado hasn't been found. My neighbor down the street from me picked up a little pup near the tornado site. He was pretty scraped up. I don't know just what a Boston bull dog looks like; but the pup that Harley has is little and he's black and white; and he's a male."

"Well, I'll be! That's the best news I've heard in two weeks! Give me Harley's number and we'll make a trip to Greenleaf. If he has Jiggs, he'll earn $25 for keeping him and I'll be glad to give you a couple of dollars, too, just for telling me about this." Daddy got the number and when we got home, Daddy explained that this man <u>might</u> have Jiggs. Daddy went to the crank phone and got the operator to place a long-distance call to Greenleaf. Thank goodness the phone lines had been repaired from the tornado damage. The conversation was brief and I was too excited to listen to it word-for-word. The man asked that we bring a picture of Jiggs for identification. It was easy to find a photo. I grabbed a picture and the leash and was ready to go. Oh, please let it be Jiggs!

Daddy couldn't drive fast enough for my liking. With each mile I felt that I was getting closer and closer to Jiggs. It had to be Jiggs! The little town of Greenleaf was a sleepy village with a grocery store and a blacksmith shop as its major occupants. I would sometimes join Daddy on a trip here to get plow-shears sharpened. Harley's street was easy to find. His white house and neatly trimmed lawn with decorative yard ornaments made me feel that he was a person who took good care of things -- and even lost pets.

Daddy went to the front door and was greeted by a friendly-looking man in his 70's. He wore bib-overalls, just like Daddy's. Things were certainly looking up. My hope was restored. "Yeah, Carl, I've been expecting you. Come down this way to the shed in the back. That's where I have him."

I couldn't contain myself. When I heard that the back shed was the place to go, I leaped out of the car and started running. I yelled in anxious anticipation. "Oh, I hope Jiggs is here!" Then loud barks came from the shed. They were music to my ears. They were the barks of Jiggs. I knew it was him!

"You know, little lady, I think you're right. I haven't heard much from the pup since I picked him up off the road; but he sure recognizes your voice." As he opened the shed door, out popped a skinny Jiggs right into my arms.

It was Jiggs, no doubt about it. He was alive and Harley had taken good care of him. There were some abrasions around his neck and ears; but the kind man had put salve on Jiggs to help him heal. "That little guy hasn't eaten very much. He's stayed in the corner and hasn't wanted to have anything to do with us. But look at him now! He's gotta be your dog! I don't need the picture to prove that he's yours."

Daddy took out his check book and wrote a check to Harley. He didn't want to take it; but Daddy insisted. Harley related the story of how he had been in Washington during the tornado and had driven west of town to look at the damage. It was near the McNitt farm that he found Jiggs. Harley said that the dog seemed like a puppy since he was so small. He didn't think a pup had a chance of survival, so he picked him up. Harley didn't get the county paper, so he hadn't read the ad. Thank goodness for the bank corner and the news that the men shared. It was how we found out about Harley and the lost dog.

"I had a feeling that the owner would show up. I told lots of people that I found a pup and I guess word gets around. Seeing your little girl and that dog together makes me certain that they belong together. It makes my heart proud." Harley was beaming.

Daddy shook Harley's hand and we all said our "Thanks". We headed back to the car. I held Jiggs tightly in my arms. What a miracle to have found him after all this time. My prayers were full of praises to God. That night was the best sleep I had gotten in two weeks. I imagine it was the same for Jiggs, as he settled down in his comfy round bed.

The tornado had wreaked havoc in our community; but people worked together to rebuild and to continue a productive life. We cared about each other and the kindness shown to all in need was remarkable. I believe God thanked me for helping the McNitts sort their silverware and photos by saving my precious pet. God sent Harley to pick up Jiggs so that the first dark night did not find him alone in the fields. God helped Harley put the salve on Jiggs to help him heal, and God had Harley spread the word that he had found a lost dog.

Momma was right when she said, "We'll find him, Rosemary." I was right, too, when I remembered the phrase: "This too shall pass." We did find Jiggs; and the sorrow of losing him did pass into a memory.

Jiggs

More Than a Bellyache!

Because I was a finicky eater, I often suffered from "tummy" problems. When I was little, Momma would have to give me "Fletcher"s Castoria" to get me on a regular track again. I didn't mind the sweet taste of this brown liquid laxative; and best of all, it worked. Roy would always tease be about my bellyaches -- saying that I was one!

When I found something that I liked to eat, I'd over-indulge. Momma made the best toll house cookies, yeast doughnuts, cinnamon rolls, and brownies. Top those off with Kool-Aid or Pepsi and I would usually come down with a growling stomach. You'd think I'd learn, but the tempting goodies were too much for my resistance. When I was eight, I found that Alka-Seltzer relieved my distress; so I'd sneak to the bathroom vanity and "plop-plop" two tablets in water. Then, B-E-L-C-H! Oh, I felt so much better; so much so that I'd steal another cookie.

One evening after supper, Daddy, Momma, and I were listening to "The Shadow" on the large console radio in the bay window area of the living room. This was a scary show and the dialogue of the mystery always ended with, "The Shadow knows." I would be frightened by the story and would ask Momma if I could sit on her lap -- something that I rarely did now that I was nine. The comfort of her arms around me made me feel safe and secure from The Shadow. When a commercial for Jello pudding came on, I recalled the delicious chocolate pudding that we had been served for supper. "Can I have the last serving of the pudding, Momma? That would be so good right now." With her approval, I went to the Servel refrigerator and retrieved the remaining pudding in a bright yellow Fiesta-ware ramekin. Back on Momma's lap with the container of velvety smooth pudding, I was content and secure to endure the rest of the mystery.

At the end of the program, I was on my way to bed. First, I had to wash the pudding dish and put it away in the cabinet. Then the usual bedtime routine was followed. Daddy had made a little jingle for me when I was little and I followed it as I got older. I even taught it to my children. "Brush your teeth and comb your hair; throw away your under wear; oh, yes, and off to bed you go." And so I did those things, brushing my teeth and washing my hands and face, and combing the "rats" out of my straight brown hair, and putting my dirty clothes in the hamper (never on the floor). Then a kiss and a hug to Daddy and Momma, and I was off to bed.

"Momma, Momma, my tummy hurts!" I held my right side as I padded into my parents' bedroom. I poked Momma on the shoulder and woke her from a sound sleep.

"What's wrong, Rosemary?" She reached to the nightstand and got a flashlight which she turned on so as not to disturb Daddy. When I told her of my pains, she gently got up from the bed and whispered, "Come to the bathroom."

We quietly left the bedroom with Daddy still making snoring sounds. In the bathroom we were able to turn on the light. It took a second for our eyes to adjust. Momma immediately got into the nursing mode that she had once done before she met Daddy. "Sit down on the side of the tub, honey. Let me take your temperature and your pulse. I also want to check your tummy. You'll have to show me where it hurts."

"Can I have an Alka-Seltzer? That usually makes me feel better." My pleading did not meet Nurse Momma's approval.

"No, dear, I don't want you to take that or any other medicine. I really don't think it's what you ate that's bothering you. It's been six hours since you've eaten. There might be other reasons why your tummy hurts." Her finger was on my wrist as she took my pulse. "Maybe you have a touch of the flu. Now hop back into bed and let me touch the place where it hurts."

I was beginning to feel better with Momma by my side. Being alone when there is pain is a scary feeling-- kinda like listening to "The Shadow" by oneself. Sharing the pain with someone you love helps diminish the hurt. I gingerly walked back to my bedroom and got into bed. When I walked, the sharp twitch in my side let me know that it was still there. I snuggled back into the crisp white sheets. It seemed cool and comforting. I lay quietly as Momma gently touched my tummy. She put her hands around my waist, then to the left side, then to the navel, then to the right side. BINGO! I cried out in pain. Momma calmly removed her hand, pulled down my pajama top, and gave me a kiss on the forehead. "You have a little kink in there. I'll put an ice pack on it and you'll feel better soon."

She went to the kitchen and I heard her open the freezer door of the Servel. Pop, pop, -- the sound of ice cubes being expelled from the freezer tray made the still, early morning come alive. Then I heard the pounding sound as she broke the large cubes into slivers so that they would fit into the narrow mouth of the hot water bottle that was to become my ice pack. She quietly floated back into my lavender room, placed the towel-wrapped pack on my right side, and covered me with a light flannel blanket. Her cool, soft hand caressed my forehead. I felt better; after all, Momma said it was only a "kink". Momma would take good care of me. What do kids do without a momma? I was so glad that Momma was here -- so glad! I fell into a deep slumber.

Muffled voices coming over the clinking of coffee cups as they came to rest on saucers, made me aware that Momma and Daddy were in the kitchen finishing a second cup of breakfast coffee. The aroma of bacon and eggs lingered in the air. It made me nauseous. I rolled to my right side, forgetting that the pain came from that area. Then, the sharp stab reminded me again that it was still there.

"I'm calling Dr. Bitzer today. He makes house calls and I'll want him to swing by here." Momma's voice was very serious. I could sense tension in the way she seemed to demand that the doctor **would** stop today.

"Don't get Doc Huntley," Daddy muttered. "He'll just give Rosemary a shot of penicillin and say, 'She's OK'." Daddy didn't like the new doc in town because of all the shots he would give his patients. Penicillin was new and Doc Huntley had a never-ending supply of it. If you had a cold -- you got penicillin. If you had an itch -- you got penicillin. No wonder all of us later developed a penicillin allergy.

Momma sensed that I was awake. "Dr. Bitzer will be here shortly. I have some sweetened hot tea for you to sip. I don't want you to eat any solid food for a while." She served the tea in one of her prettiest Bavarian china cups. I only got to use such a cup when I was sick in bed. That way the precious heirloom china, with its delicate pink roses, didn't have a chance of falling on the floor -- only onto a goose down comforter!

Dr. Bitzer was a roly-poly man in his 50's. His dark hair was always oiled down over the top of his round head. It looked as if he were wearing a patent-leather skull cap. In contrast, his thin mustache consisted of coarse, dry hair -- not at all shiny like the hair on his head. I wondered why he didn't oil it, too.

"So, Rosemary, you're not feeling well this morning. Let me take a look at you." Dr. Bitzer opened his weathered black leather medical satchel. Since I had been enthralled by the use of his hair pomade, why hadn't he oiled the old leather kit, too? What a stupid thing to think about at a time like this. I was sick and my mind was filled with dumb, trivial thoughts.

Dr. Bitzer's medical kit emitted an aroma of alcohol and iodine as he reached for his stethoscope. The instrument was cold, as was this early April morning. "Heart and lungs sound good." Then he felt my neck and had me open my mouth and say "Ahh.". So far so good, until it came to the belly.

"Where does it hurt?" he inquired.

"Right here" -- as I put my fingers to the right side of my tummy and radiating near the right hip bone.

"Let's check it out", and with that, he poked to the left, in the middle, and then to the right; just like Momma had done in the early morning.

When he pressed on the right side I immediately yelled, "Ouch! That's where it really hurts!" I didn't want any more poking.

Nodding his oily head up and down, Dr. Bitzer turned his attention to Momma. "Looks like we have an inflamed appendix here. The ice packs have helped control the pain and she's not running a fever, so perhaps it's a situation that will subside in time. However, Clara, that little piece of gut could get abscessed again with a more serious infection and a possible rupture could occur. I think we need to take action to prevent this from happening."

"Oh, Doctor, I agree. I know all about the seriousness of this. My mother had such an incident." Then her voice became a muffled whisper as she talked to the doctor. I knew what she was talking about because I had been told of Grandma Meyrose dying from a ruptured appendix. Oh, boy! Was I about to die?

Washington, Kansas did not have a hospital; so the nearest one was at Clay Center, my birthplace eight years earlier. Would it also be my death place? Again, my mind was racing. I would have been better off thinking about the doctor's hair.

"Let me contact the hospital and set up a surgical time." Dr. Bitzer was all business as he went to the wall phone, rang for the Operator, and directed the call to the Clay Center Hospital for Dr. Cruson.

Momma came back to my bedside and said that the operation would take care of this pain that I had experienced. It was far more than an ordinary bellyache. It was appendicitis.

Dr. Bitzer was successful in getting Dr. Cruson and the surgery ward for later in the afternoon. The trip of only 25 miles was fairly easy, except when it came to bumps and railroad tracks. Daddy tried to take it easy and I'd hold my side to cushion the pain that stabbed beneath the ice pack.

When we arrived at the hospital, they were expecting us. All kinds of questions were asked of Momma and Daddy while I was whisked away to an examining room. Vital statistics were taken along with blood and urine samples. I had never had blood drawn before, and I had never had to "pee in a cup" before. I learned that I was being "prepped" for surgery. A whole new list of medical terms was being bantered about: "CBC", "OR", "PREP", and "STAT" -- it was as if I had entered a foreign country and I didn't speak the language.

It was wise that Momma hadn't given me solid food. Since I needed surgery, it was good that I had an empty stomach. My white blood count was elevated, an indication that my body was fighting the infection. With ice packs on my right side, I was made comfortable in a big hospital bed with metal barriers on each side. I was the only patient in a big room that was painted green (institutional green like all public buildings used). There was another bed in the room, but it was empty. Since I was the only child patient in the surgery unit, they never roomed adults and children together. The coldness of the room with its tile floor made it seem like a cell.

Momma and Daddy were with me as the nurses came back for more vital signs. I was really thirsty and asked for a drink of water. All I was allowed were ice chips. Maybe I could sneak the melted ice out of the ice packs that were on my right side; but Momma gave me an emphatic, "No". Looking back, I don't believe I was the easiest patient to handle.

The soft whispered conversation between Daddy and Momma lulled me to sleep. I didn't want to miss their talk, but I did. I was awakened by the "swish-swish" sound of nurses' shoes followed by a "click, click" of another person entering the room. Standing over me was a tall, gray-haired man wearing a white lab coat and a stethoscope around his neck. "Hello, Rosemary. I'm Dr. Cruson and I'm going to help you feel better soon. I'm going to make a tiny cut on the right side of your belly, take that nasty appendix out, stitch you up, and send you back to the farm in a few days. We'll put you in a deep sleep, so you won't feel the cut." Then he leaned closer and whispered, "I'll make the cut so small that you'll be able to be a fan dancer when you get older." His gentle voice and his smile made me trust him. However, I didn't really aspire to become a fan dancer like Sally Rand, a noted entertainer who was currently scheduled to play at the Kansas State Fair. I just wanted the pain to go away.

Dr. Cruson, wearing brown leather loafers, "clicked" his way out to the hall and he beckoned for Momma and Daddy to join him. He wanted to be more explicit and there were probably things that these little ears shouldn't hear.

In the meantime, two nurses were getting me ready for surgery. A gurney (another new word for me) was brought in and I was able to scoot myself onto it. A nurse covered me with light-weight blankets and belted me on the portable bed. Momma and Daddy kissed me and said that they were going to watch the operation from the observation room over-looking the surgical table. They would be near-by and that made me feel better. "Swish, swish", the nurses pushed me along, followed by the "tap and click" of Momma's heels and "plop, plop" of Daddy's brogans.

The OR was cold and very bright. A huge round light was overhead and I was transferred to the operation table and covered with green sheets. They really liked the color green here -- not my favorite color.

At the head of the table, a man wearing a mask, told me to "Take deep breaths" as he put a white cone over my nose and mouth. "This will make you sleepy. Count backwards from 10 to 1."

I took a deep breath in and another breath out. I repeated the breaths and began counting: "10, 9, 8, 7,6,..5,...4.....3.......". I was inhaling ether, a terrible smelling liquid. My sense of hearing changed. I heard echoes reverberating and the huge light began moving closer and closer. I felt as if I were being closed in. I reared up trying to make my escape, only to be pushed down rapidly and given more ether. Now the overhead light and a character that looked like Mickey Mouse were coming down on me again! A jumble of sounds came to my ears. "Hold her down", "More ether", "I started the cut!" . . . . .then silence. I was out.

I awoke back in the room where I was placed earlier in the day. Nurses were at my bedside along with Momma and Daddy. I was groggy and very thirsty. I had a bad taste in my mouth and a burning sensation in my nose. I felt like I had been on a long journey and I wanted to be at home with a big glass of water to quench my thirst. Please, may I have some water? Please! But only ice chips would be given to me.

Then the misery began. I got sick to my stomach. There was nothing to expel, as I hadn't eaten any solid food; but I retched up horrible bile and stomach juices that were awful tasting. The nurse told me that ether could cause the stomach upset and since I had a double-dose of it, I would probably be nauseated for quiet a while. She was right. I was sick all night and part of the next day. There was nothing in my stomach; but I puked and puked anyway.

Momma stayed with me all night; while Daddy drove back home to check on the animals. I was so glad to have her with me to hold my head as I vomited into the emesis pan, to wipe my head with a cool cloth, and to speak gentle words. How could I ever live without her?

Later in the afternoon, one day after the surgery, my upset stomach was finally settled. No more vomiting! My eyes were heavy and my chest was sore from all the vomiting. I fell into a deep sleep. When I awoke, Momma was by my side with a tray that held my supper: apple juice, red Jello, and more ice chips. I was cautioned by the nurse to "Take it slow". I did! I certainly didn't want to get sick again.

I began to feel more alive with food and liquid in my tummy. My thoughts now centered on my operation site, so I gingerly felt the right side of my abdomen where bulky pads cushioned the area. I gently pushed -- it didn't hurt! Dr. Cruson got the culprit out.

I was ordered to stay in bed. I couldn't get up to use the bathroom, so I had to use a bed pan for toilet duties. I really hated the stainless steel monster that was slid under my bottom. It was always cold. The chill kinda took the urge "to go" out of my mind. Why couldn't I get up and walk; or why couldn't they give me a warm bed pan? I would have to wait for the third day before I could get out of bed with a nurse by my side to assist me.

Momma had rented a room in a home nearby so that she could be near me. That meant so much to me because the days got very long. Nurses were "swish-swishing" around to tend to other patients and they seldom came to my room unless they needed to take vital signs. There were no such modern conveniences like TV or radio in the rooms as there are today. I was very lonesome. I'd listen intently for sounds and foot steps as they approached my room. These sounds told me just who was passing by my room: "click, click" (that's a doctor), "clomp, clomp", (that's a visitor), "jingle, jingle" (that's the janitor making his cleaning rounds). Finally, "tap-click, tap-click" -- the sound of Momma walking toward my room in her high heels. What a wonderful sound. How glad I was to see her.

She'd read stories to me. My favorite book was **The Gateway to Storyland.** I asked her to read the stories over and over. I never tired of them, but I imagine that she did. I really liked the story of Rumpelstilskin. As I would brush my short brown hair, I'd quote: "Rapunsel, Rapunsel, let down your hair." About the fourth day after surgery, I noticed that when I brushed my hair, my brush would be loaded with strands of hair. My thick brown hair was getting thinner! Oh, my, -- would I be bald like Daddy? If brushing made my hair come out, then I wouldn't brush. However, I noticed an abundance of hair on the pillowcases even without my brushing. My hair was coming out all by itself! The nurse told me that this was another side effect of the heavy ether dosage. I wouldn't lose all my hair at once, so I wouldn't be bald; and it would grow back (that's what the nurse told me). In the weeks to follow, the nurse was correct. My hair did grow back. This time it came back with a natural wave in it. No more stick-straight hair from now on. I was lucky-- but then I did pay the price.

On the seventh day, I was released from the hospital to go home. I'd have to return in three days to get the stitches out. It was wonderful to be wheeled out of the hospital into the crisp April air. Everything looked so new and fresh. This time the color green was a treat to see.

At home I had to take it easy. Our dog, Jiggs, had to "stay down" even though he was so excited to see me. He had missed our playing. I had missed it too. I had missed the swinging in the tree swing and I cautiously sat down to go back and forth a few times. My right side felt tight and sore. I decided I better obey and take it easy.

After three days, we made the return trip to the hospital. This time I was taken to an examining room where Dr. Cruson joined us. He was pleased with my recovery and said that I had done very well. "Now let's get those pesky stitches out so that you won't feel the tightness anymore. I'll snip the cat-gut and you'll be on your way."

"Are the stitches really made of cat-gut?" He merely smiled as he snipped and released the stitches. He never really answered my question.

The very last stitch -- the one at the bottom of the incision -- released with a pin-dot of blood in its wake. Dr. Cruson immediately took his gloved hand and placed an alcohol pad on it. "Keep the incision dry and covered. I doubt if the last stitch causes Rosemary any trouble; but if it does, consult Dr. Bitzer and he'll know what to do."

He was addressing all of this to Momma. Then he leaned down and looked me in the eyes, smiled, and whispered, "You'll still be able to be a fan dancer if you want!" With that, he removed his gloves, shook hands with me and then with Momma and Daddy. Then he turned and "clicked" out of the room.

It's a good thing that I didn't aspire to be a fan dancer. That pesky last stitch didn't heal properly. Momma took me to see Dr. Bitzer at his office above the First National Bank in Washington. There was no elevator, so we had to make the trek of 20 or more steps. By the time I reached the landing, my side hurt with a pulling sensation.

The office was warm in the May heat. The windows were open, and oscillating fans blew the air back and forth. Sounds from the street below could be heard. How I wished that I was down there and not in this office. A strong rubbing alcohol scent was in the air; but at least it wasn't ether.

Dr. Bitzer's nurse helped me into a gown and guided me up the footstool to get on the examining table. A crisp linen sheet felt cool as I laid back. Dr. Bitzer, with his oily black hair, looked even greasier on this warm Saturday afternoon. The heat was getting to him; and with his hair pomade and his perspiration, he seemed like a plump meat ball.

"Looks like we have a case of "proud flesh" here. We'll cauterize this. It should heal nicely." His statement was in a matter-of-fact way. He directed his nurse to prepare a tray that held a white ceramic oblong dish in a stainless steel heating element. Long wooden swabs with cotton buds on the ends were at the side. Dr. Bitzer put on rubber gloves and told me to "lie very still". Momma was on one side of me and the nurse on the other. They would hold me down as the long swab, which had been dipped into the hot mixture, was swirled around in the wound. Oh, my! This was about as painful as the appendicitis attack. I didn't ever want to go through that again.

But sometimes things don't work out like we want them to. The above scenario was played out every Saturday during the months of May, June, July, and part of August. I hated to get my bandage changed daily. I'd ask Momma if the seepage would ever stop. It was persistent, meaning that the infection was still present. "We can't give up", Momma would say. Of course I also heard her favorite saying: "This too shall pass."

Every Saturday was a depressing and hurtful time for me. I know Daddy and Momma were worried, too. Even Dr. Cruson was consulted and he agreed with the course of treatment that was being followed. I wondered why this was called "proud flesh"; there certainly wasn't anything prideful about it. After months of treatment and a long summer spent being inactive, the menace was eventually conquered, leaving a deep hole in my abdomen on the lower right side. Often a new physician will ask me if I had suffered a bullet wound. I merely smile and reply, "No, just an infected stitch that ruined my chance of putting Sally Rand out of business."

Life Lessons

Life on the farm was filled with many life lessons. Where else could a person find first-hand examples of planting and harvesting, nurturing and caring, life and death? I watched Daddy plant seeds into the fertile ground and saw them raise their tiny heads toward the Kansas sun. With the luck of the elements, a crop could grow to be harvested; or it could be ruined by a hail storm or a drought. I grew up knowing that the weather was an important element -- one to be taken seriously. Our personal safety, along with the safety of the livestock, was of foremost importance; but our concerns were also for the crops in the field. Perhaps that's why I remember the saying: "Save for a rainy day" because every farmer had to save for a day when the weather might destroy the crop which would be the farmer's income.

We raised livestock and chickens as a source of food and income. I recall the time a little chick was being pecked in the rear-end by the other chicks. Momma said that this often happened when the pin feathers were sprouting out of the fluffy yellow fuzz of new hatchlings. She would put a purple medicine in the glass water fountains to control the outbreak of coxsidiosis and the urge for the chicks to peck each other to death.

I couldn't understand the cruelty of it. To see a little chick cornered by the others made me mad. I captured one innocent victim and asked Momma if I could raise him. "Rosemary, I know you mean well, but this will be a lot of work for you to watch this little chick and keep him in a penned area away for the others. If he survives, he will have to go to market or be on our table. These creatures are our livelihood -- not pets."

"I know, Momma; but let me try. He's so cute and I think I can keep him alive." I nestled the fuzzy yellow chick in my hands and looked at the reddened skin where the others had pecked. Momma told me to apply some tar compound to help heal the area. When I did, he looked funny with a "black bottom"; but he seemed to sense that I was caring for him. I created a separate area in the brooder house away from the rest of the flock where my little charge could be by himself, yet warmed by the brooder stove. I was going to be his care-giver. I named him "Petey Joe".

This was the first living thing that I was to have sole care for in my lifetime. Many others were to follow; but "Petey Joe" was special. He became attached to me and would follow me around the farm when I took him out of the brooder house. He seemed to strut because he was allowed out of the prison, while the other chicks had to remain penned up in the fenced brooder house area. Both Momma and Daddy warned me not to get too attached to this chicken. I tried not to, but of course I did. What pride I took in that little bird! He became strong and healthy; and I felt that I had been his rescuer. I took pictures of him. One picture showed him at six weeks old weighing 1½ pounds -- just about the size for eating!

I couldn't watch the slaughter or the preparation of "Petey Joe" to become our Sunday dinner; but I recall that this chicken was the BEST chicken that I had ever eaten. We all agreed and would often comment on this when other birds were consumed. "Sure isn't as good as 'Petey Joe.'" I like to think that it was due to the fact that this chicken, with my help, was saved for a purpose and he fulfilled it. I believe that all 4-H kids feel this pride about their livestock. As farmers, we raise the animals and birds as a food source. When we succeed, we're filled with grief-stricken pride.

Another one of my charges was "Porky", a little runt of a pig. The large litter pushed him aside as he tried to nurse. Daddy said that the little guy didn't have a chance. When I heard that news, I was immediately up to the challenge. "I did a good job with "Petey Joe", could I bottle feed this little pig and see if he'll eat for me?"

"Yes, you did very well with that chicken, but a pig has to stay in the pen with its mother. I don't want you near that pen because the sow will protect her piglets. Maybe this is nature's way of culling out the weak ones." Daddy was very logical and probably right; but I always had a way of wrangling my way with him.

"If you brought him up to the house when he needs to be fed, I could have a bottle of warm milk and a nipple on it so that he could drink. Then when he's finished, you could return him to the pen to his mother. I bet he'd take the milk." I was anxious to begin my chore as a wet-nurse to a pig. He was tiny and cute. His little pink nose and his beady black eyes made the rest of his pink body seem so small. He seemed more like a toy instead of an animal. He needed nourishment; he needed me! Guess what? Daddy gave in!

As the weeks passed, it was fun to play nurse to "Porky". I'd wrap him in a flannel blanket and pretent that he was a baby. My dog, Jiggs, liked the fact that I was giving attention to the pig instead of dressing him up in doll clothes. "Porky" began to thrive and he was soon on his own in the pigpen.

I had the smelly job of slopping the piglets now that they were older. Slop was any left-over food from our table. It always had a peculiar smell, depending on the various scraps. Put together sour milk, stale bread, vegetables, potato peelings, apple cores, and you have an interesting mixture. Whenever I neared the pen, "Porky" knew me and was the first in line. What a pig he was; but I was proud that he made his way past the others who were once so greedy at mealtime. Again, I had rescued a little animal from almost certain premature death.

One morning I was late in getting up. I had to dress for school and I had to slop the hogs. I put on a pretty blue cotton dress with pin-tucks in the front. It was crisp and clean and I liked wearing it. When "Porky" saw me, he made a dash to the fence and knocked the slop bucket forward toward me instead of into the trough. My pristine dress was laden with soaked bread, sour milk, oatmeal, and left-overs from supper. I was really mad at "Porky". When Momma heard my screams, she came running to the pen. "Don't get upset with him; he has become a strong and eager eater. You were late this morning and he was only anxious to get his food." She was right. "Porky" was on his way to becoming a prize pig. He wasn't a runt any more. As for me and my dress, I washed off the slop and quickly changed into clean clothes and hurried on my way to school.

To my friends who lived in town, they felt that it was cruel to slaughter my animals. "How could you do that to a pet?" I explained to them that these animals were livestock and I knew that they were raised either for food or income. They weren't really pets; but they did hold special places in my heart.

New life was always evident on a farm. My first opportunity to see a live birth came about when our mother cat had a litter of kittens on the side porch just off the kitchen. Momma always fed "Kitty" some scraps of food; but "Kitty" was a barn cat. Being a mouser, she was to get her main meals from her catches. One day I commented on how fat "Kitty" was getting. "She's going to have kittens," Momma replied. Of course this started the questions about how that came about. Momma was good at explaining things; and in a matter-of-fact way, I was given my first lesson in sex education. Now I had a vague idea of how kittens, puppies, calves, and human babies came into being. Those were the categories of infants that I had noticed in my short life-time.

However, I was in for a real shock about birth when I opened the porch door one morning to find "Kitty" on a braided throw rug having something exiting her body. The slimy, sack-encased object looked foreign to me. "Momma, Momma, come here! 'Kitty' is in trouble."

Momma came to see what the problem was. "She's OK. She's having her babies. Each kitten is in a sack and the mother will break the sack and lick it clean with her tongue. Then another baby will be born and the same process will start over until all the babies are out of her body. Let's gently move her out of the walk-way. I don't want you to disturb yer. She has a lot of work ahead of her and she can't get down to the barn yet. I don't want you to scare her. Come inside and watch through the kitchen window. Be very quiet." Momma was gentle as she picked up the rug and moved it along with the mother cat to a safe corner.

I was in awe at the event that played out before me through the window. It was a miracle -- one that I had never seen before. Just as Momma said, "Kitty" broke the sack on each kitten and licked it clean -- all five of them. That seemed like a "yucky" duty; but it had to be done so that the kittens could breathe. Then she cleaned herself and nestled her young-ones to her breasts. After bobbling around in a blind frenzy, they latched on for their first breakfast.

During the remainder of the day, I was glued to the kitchen window. I didn't use the porch door to go outside; instead, I used the front door. Jiggs and I kept our distance from the new mother, just as Momma had ordered.

The next morning I awoke thinking that the kittens would be big enough to play. Boy, was I disappointed to see that their eyes were still closed and their fur was still matted. Then I was shocked to see that one kitten was missing. "What happened to one kitten? It's not here. Did Jiggs get it?"

"No, I believe 'Kitty' is in the process of moving her litter to the nest that she has undoubtedly prepared in the barn -- probably in the hayloft. She knows that a busy porch is not the place to raise kittens. I think nature played a trick on her and she had her babies earlier that she expected." Momma was setting out a few scraps for "Kitty" because the new mother cat needed to keep up her strength for the milk production that she would have to provide.

"Can I go down to the barn and find the nest?" I curiously pleaded.

"Absolutely not! You stay away from the cat or she'll have to move them again. If that be the case, she might lose some of her babies. You wouldn't want the innocent little creatures to die, would you?" Putting it in morbid terms, Momma convinced me to stay away from the barn and the hiding place. As the day progressed, I noticed that "Kitty" had moved the other four to their secret home. In the following weeks, I was always on the lookout for the five little kittens.

One morning as I was tending to my duties of collecting eggs from the hen house, I wandered up to the barn. I heard a rustle in the hay as I approached; then out popped a yellow kitten playing with his gray-and-white sibling. When they saw me, they immediately darted for cover. I was so excited. I had found the kittens! I rushed back to the house to put the fresh eggs on the kitchen table. Then I excitely returned to the barn only to find it quiet ,with no trace of kittens anywhere.

The next morning I went to the barn before doing my daily chores. This time I was very quiet. I tip-toed into the barn; and like a spy, I looked around to find the five rascals. There they were -- one yellow, one gray-and white, two totally gray, and the other was a muckled brown color. They were playing tag with each other and rolling around in the hay. When the yellow one spotted me, he immediately stopped, raised his tail, and hissed out at me. The others followed suit and then dashed under the milk stanchions to get away from the giant intruder.

It took many days before the kittens would make their appearance again. "Kitty" returned to the porch for her daily scraps and eventually she was followed by her five little ones. They weren't friendly at first, but in time they got to know me and the ball of twine that I temptingly rolled toward them. I felt a closeness to them because I had seen them enter the world.

I believe that these life lessons formed a caring attitude that I have embraced throughout my life. I have been called to care for others; and I have never reneged on doing so. It has been a very big part of my life. How wonderful to see live births. Thanks to my dear adopted daughter, Michele, I have witnessed the births of her two darling children, Emily and Emmet. Each time the awe, the wonder, and the thrill were present -- just like it was with the birth of the kittens. Birth is truly a miracle from God!

Then came the day when illness and death struck our family. Another life lesson for another chaper.

A Heavenly Sign

    I was close to my grandparents. Being their only "blood" grandchild, I meant the world to them. I saw them daily when I'd join Daddy to drive down to "the creek" -- that's what Daddy called the 100 acre farm on the banks of Ash Creek. There were always hugs and treats waiting for me. If I planned to go to town later in the day, Grandpa would always give me a smile as he slipped a dime in my hand. In those days a dime could buy a bag of candy, a soda, a comic book, or hair ribbons. It was fun to have my very own money!
    I felt the closeness that Daddy had with his parents. He'd visit with them every day. Of course, the distance of two miles was not a great one, so it was easy to make the trip. The care and concern that he had for them made me want to honor my parents the way he honored his. I had the feeling that Grandpa, Grandma, Daddy, and Momma would live forever.
    Then one day, Daddy was very solemn as he told me that Grandma was ill. Grandpa had taken her to the doctor, and Dr. LeMaster advised them to go to the Mayo Clinic in Rochester, Minnesota. I didn't know exactly what was wrong; but I knew that it was serious. Arrangements were made for Grandpa and Grandma to take a Trailways Bus for the journey. Before she left, Grandma wrote a letter to all of us "in the event that I do not return". I gave her a special hug and I noticed tears in her eyes. "It'll be OK, Grandma. I just know it." I had no idea of her medical problem; but I did feel that she would return to us. She had to!

The days passed slowly for us. Grandpa called daily to let us know what was happening. He was doing all right in the big city of Rochester. He even sent us a postcard that a street photographer had taken as he was walking along on his way to the clinic. He seemed handsome and determined as he strode by in his dress coat and fedora. He wasn't wearing the usual farm gear of over-alls that I was so accustomed to seeing him wear.

Grandma endured many tests and at the completion of them, sobering news was to follow. CANCER! Both of her breasts were involved and a double mastectomy was to be performed. The doctors were optimistic about her recovery and we had faith and hope in them and in God. Surgery was completed and after two more weeks, she was able to come back home. Fortunately, Momma had nursing knowledge, and she was able to change bandages and help Grandma do the needed exercises to get her mobility and arm movements back. I never saw her wounds, but I did notice how flat-chested she was (just like my 9 year old body). I never knew the contents of the letter that she had written before her treatment in Rochester. Perhaps it was discarded or hidden in the family Bible. I didn't need to know. She was home and I was happy to be with her again. Nothing else mattered.

Slowly, Grandma gained her strength and she was able to do her housework and cooking. Things seemed to be going fine for about a year. Then she noticed small nodules all over her body and she was becoming more and more fatigued. This time her local doctor diagnosed her with another outbreak of cancer that was throughout her body.

All through the summer of 1947, she remained in bed for the biggest span of time. Momma would insist that she sit up briefly and then repositon herself when she got back in bed. Grandma was miserable -- unable to eat or drink because she couldn't keep it down. Then the Kansas heat was unbearable in July and August. This was before air-conditioning. We did have REA, so an electric fan oscillated back and forth. On really hot days, Daddy would get 50 pounds of ice, put it in a metal wash tub, and position the fan behind it. What a wonderful cool and refreshing breeze it created.

That summer was spent at Grandma's bedside. We all knew that the disease was a serious and deadly one. The chances of Grandma living much longer were very slim; so we made the most of each day. I'd color pictures for her, read books to her, and sing to her. She'd always join me in singing "Zip-a-dee-do-dah". Momma told me that when Grandma nodded off, I was to quietly leave the room and let her rest.

The days were very long as we spent time down at "the creek" My imaginary friends were left at my house. I did have Rags, my buddy from past years; but he had grown older and he was now bonded to Grandpa. He wasn't interested in my childhood games of hide-and-seek and retrieve the stick. I busied myself with reading and drawing pictures.

Then one day I realized that Momma's birthday was coming up in July. I had to get her something; but I wanted it to be a surprise. If I went to town with Momma and Daddy and purchased something, then the surprise element would be gone. I felt that I should make her something, so I sneaked around Grandma's house and found some lovely cotton fabric in a bottom dresser drawer. There was also some cotton batting. I came up with a great idea --I'd make Momma a potholder. So every afternoon when Grandma slept and Momma tended duties of the house, I secretly retreated to the back bedroom and gathered the material, scissors, needle and thread, and my design for a lovely butterfly potholder.

I cut into pink, purple, yellow and blue fabrics. I selected embroidery floss and outlined my design on the top of my project. Day after day, I diligently stitched and padded the 8x8 square; I could see my plan coming to fruition. Needless to say, I was very proud of my project. I even found a metal ring to put in the corner of the project so that it could hang near the kitchen stove. On July 11, I presented my tissue-wrapped gift to Momma. She was delighted as well as surprised. "Where did you get this beautiful fabric, Rosemary?"

I hesitantly responded, "Oh, I found it in the bottom dresser drawer in the front bedroom."

" Oops! I think you found some quilt material of Grandma's. I hope things aren't cut-up too much -- but you did a wonderful job on this potholder." Momma traced the embroidery that created the form of a butterfly with her finger. She was pleased that I had remembered her special day amid all the confusion of Grandma's illness.

When Grandma studied my handicraft, she beamed. "You did the stitches that I taught you very well. You'll have to make one for me" Of course I knew that she didn't expect to ever use a potholder again; but it was a wonderful compliment that she liked my work. She also reassured me that using the quilt fabric was allright with her.

Momma must have treasured it too, as she kept it on a special hook near the oven. As for the cut-up fabric, I believe it was salvageable for quilt projects at a later time. I know that I should have asked permission before using the material; but the surprise element would have been destroyed. Momma never scolded me about my piracy. I think the whole episode was a welcomed diversion.

The days passed slowly. I often wondered why none of the neighbors came to visit her. In fact, many of the neighbors shunned us on Saturday market days. A quick, "Hello, Clara", or "Hello, Carl", would be about the only greeting we'd get. One time I asked Momma why that was. "People are afraid of the word **cancer**. They think it's contagious; but it isn't. I wish they knew that they would be safe to visit Mary; it would mean so much to her. But we can't change minds, so we have to do the best and spend time with Grandma. She loves your company -- so who needs the neighrbors?" It made me feel so proud that I was doing a good job taking care of Grandma and helping my Momma,too. Her words made me feel so important.

As Grandma became weaker, a private nurse was hired to care for her in the late afternoon and all through the night. That allowed all of us to get some rest.

"Grandma's going to die, isn't she?" I asked one evening as I was saying my prayers.

"Yes, Rosemary, you're right. Grandma has put up a good fight, but her body is wearing out. We'll all be sad, and we'll miss her; but God has a better place for her in Heaven." She made it seem that the "better place" was a blessing instead of being in a bedroom with the stifling hot Kansas heat.

"I thought you were going to say, "This too shall pass." You have always told me that whenever I have been sad. Remember when we lost Jiggs? That's what you said. I think I like that phrase better now because when Grandma gets to Heaven, her cancer will pass and she'll be OK."

"That's exactly what it means, Rosemary. All things, good or bad, change. This bad time for Grandma will soon change. Many cancer patients that I have known pass away in September. Kinda like the falling of the leaves in autumn. Maybe that's when Grandma will pass. Close your eyes now and think of happy thoughts about Grandma. She loves you so much." Momma opened the side door to my room to let the evening breeze blow in from the window. As the filmy white curtains blew back and forth in the breeze, I thought of all the things about Grandma that I loved -- her smile, her laugh, her chicken and dumplings, her cherry pies, her putting her wrists under cold running water when the days were hot. I fell asleep. I bet I had a smile on my face.

Dorothy was called to come in from Wichita. "Grandma is dying." Roy and his wife, Ginny, lived in an apartment in town; so they were near-by. Grandma was alert and happy to see everyone; but the visits couldn't last very long. She was constantly vomiting and that made her weaker and weaker. I remember Grandpa taking the emesis pan out and digging holes in the sandy soil to bury the waste. Perhaps he was afraid that people would think that this waste could cause cancer. He felt better by burying it.

It was nine o'clock in the evening when Daddy got a call that Grandma was nearing death. Her physician had been called. Dorothy had left earlier in the week to return to work; but Roy and Ginny had been with us for supper and they were sitting and visiting, when we got the call. Daddy didn't want me to be at Grandma's bedside. He asked Ginny to stay with me and help me get to bed at a decent time. I liked Ginny, and I knew we would get along just fine. The others left for "the creek" and I got ready for bed.

Ginny let me use some of her perfume after I had taken a bath. I really smelled good! The September evening was warm; so we pushed the bed near the open window. Ginny raised the blind to let in the panoramic view of the starry sky. Crickets and tree frogs made a night-time symphony and we quietly talked about Grandma and Heaven. We counted the stars in the big dipper and noticed clusters of tiny stars that clung together.

"I wonder what Heaven's like. Are the streets lined with gold?"

"Oh, Rosemary, I haven't a clue. I know that the Bible says it will be a glorious place. At least there will be no pain in Heaven. That will be so good that Garndma Mary will be free of her cancer." Then Ginny moved closer to me and pointed outside. "Let's look for falling stars." It was getting late; but neither of us wanted to sleep. Our minds were on Grandma.

Was it a premoniton that prompted Ginny to want to look for a falling star? I don't know. "When Grandma dies, will there be a shooting star to tell us of the event? It might be like the star of Bethlehem when Jesus was born." I studied the sky and pondered my question. I didn't expect Ginny to answer. I was merely thinking out loud.

Then to our amazement, a huge shooting star sailed across the sky. "Do you suppose that is for Grandma?" Ginny looked at the bedside clock -- 12:49 AM. It was the only shooting star that we saw that evening. My, it was late --later than I had ever stayed up ; I was tired and succumbed to sleep. Ginny quietly stole out of the room and waited for the others to return.

The following morning, I was awakened by voices in the kitchen. Roy and Ginny had returned from their apartment in town and joined Momma and Daddy for breakfast. Serious talk about Grandma and arrangements could be heard. "Ward's funeral home will provide good service." "I think Mom would like it there and not at the church." "We need to call the florist." "Don't you think Monday morning would be a good time for the service?" "Yes, and burial at Rock Cemetery will be in the afternoon." "I'll call Dorothy and let her know before she goes to work today. I wonder if she can take a long week-end off." Chatter, chatter. Everyone was talking at once. No one heard me patter in the room.

"Did Grandma die?" Tears flooded my eyes before an answer came. How silly to ask when I overheard things about flowers, funerals, and burials. I guess grief makes a person stupid -- at least it did me! Then I asked a question in which the answer has always astounded me. "When did Grandma die?"

Daddy looked at me in a quizzical way. "I think the doctor wrote down 12:45 AM on the death certificate. Why in the world would you think of that?"

I looked over at Ginny. Both of us smiled and remembered the starry night and the falling star that sped across the sky at 12:49 AM -- that was the sign that I had hoped would be the announcement that Grandma had entered Heaven. When we related the story, everyone was silent. We all felt that Grandma Mary Dague had made a safe journey. The date was September 9, 1947

The autumn morning was cool and crisp. Ironically, now that she was gone, the sweltering heat gave way to sunny, clear skies and winds that reminded us that fall and winter were ahead. The funeral home was filled with flowers from relatives and neighbors who now sent their wishes. How come they couldn't have visited her when she was alive and lonely for companionship? I suppose they thought that the embalming fluid washed away all the cancer and that they'd be safe. I had to stop myself from thinking those mean thoughts. Our friends and neighbors were nice and Grandpa needed their comfort now more than ever.

Grandma looked so good in the casket. She was dressed in her favorite purple dress and her bobbed gray hair had a lovely sheen to it. She looked like her usual healthy self in her "Sunday best". I was glad to see her look that way. I don't remember any more details about the funeral except one. Her favorie hymn, "In the Garden" was sung by the soloist. It was beautiful and it reminded me of Grandma in her garden of peonies, zinnias, snap-dragons, iris, and holly-hocks. When I hear the refrains of that song today, I recall her funeral and the first family loss that I had in my life. Death is always hard to take. We want to live forever; but then would we want to live forever with cancer or any other debilitating disease?

Grandma was healed of her cancer. She was in Heaven and she was happy. I bet she was singing "Zip-a-dee-do-dah"-- I was singing it too!

God Loves Me

One Sunday morning Momma announced that we were going to church. I can't recall if I had been particularly bad and needed salvation; or if Momma thought it was time for me to know the Lord. After Grandma's death and the sign of the falling star, I was finding myself thinking and talking about God and Heaven. Because Daddy and Momma hadn't gone to church, I was surprised by this sudden news. Daddy declined the invitation to join us. "I had enough church when I was a little boy. Never liked the rich elders jingling money in their pockets and then cheating their fellow man the next day. I bet the same thing goes on today. I don't object to you girls going; but I'll stay home and talk to the Lord here."

Momma had not grown up with a religious background. An unpleasant experience occurred in her childhood when her mother, Nellie, tried to get help from the Catholic Church in regard to her drunken husband. Whenever Nellie asked for guidance from the priest, she was rebuffed and told, "If you were a better wife, your husband would not have to drink."

Often Nellie would hide her little girl, Clara, in the woodshed behind the house whenever her husband was on a drinking binge. One evening when Nellie met her drunken husband at the top of the stairs, she warded off his advances and pushed him away. He tumbled down the stairs and sprawled out in a coma or stupor at the bottom of the steps. He remained there throughout the night and Nellie wondered if he were dead or in a coma. The next morning he finally stirred. Nellie breathed a sigh of relief; not because he was alive, but because she hadn't accidentally killed him. She knew right then and there that she would divorce him, no matter what the Catholic Church had to say. She had to protect her daughter from the drunken abuse that would surely continue. Of course, Nellie was ex-communicated and lived out her days without the solace of formal religion. She did believe in God; but she couldn't believe in the Catholic faith and their doctrines. On her own, she taught her daughter to believe in God, Jesus, and the Holy Spirit.

Momma confided in me that she had been afraid of her father. One minute he was kind and loving; the next minute he could be in a rage. As a young child, she had also been scared to be out in the woodshed all by herself. I suppose she was glad when her mother decided to divorce her father. Later, Nellie remarried to a man who did not drink. Momma said that her step-father was very kind and compassionate.

With that background, Momma set out to find a church -- one that would accept her Catholic baptism. She found such acceptance in the Presbyterian Church. And so it was that Momma and I would go to church every Sunday with the Presbyterians. They needed more enrollees, so the two of us were warmly welcomed. We became regular church-goers because if we missed a Sunday, Rev. Rose, the minister, would make a house call. Momma would often laugh and say, "If we want to keep the minister away, we better go to church." He was a nice man; but sometimes we just didn't want unexpected company.

Rev. Rose was a retired evangelist from the road circuit. He was a thin, dashing man, about 6 feet tall with silver white hair. His wife was a tiny lady with flame red hair that came directly from a bottle. They had become tired of traveling from town to town and setting up tents. They wanted to settle down in their older years. When the Presbyterians in Washington, Kansas needed a minister, he signed up for the job. I doubt if he was a Presbyterian; but then it didn't matter to the small town congregation. Besides, he gave a robust sermon and his wife could play all 88 keys on the piano with a flourish. I particularly liked the hymn that began: "Rouse them, soldiers, rally 'round the banner. Ready, steady, pass the word along …." Often Rev. Rose would begin the Sunday gathering with that song. With the Bible in one hand raised over his silver head, he'd march down the aisle and up to the pulpit singing at the top of his voice. It certainly woke up everyone and got us ready to listen to his message. With the lessons from the Bible and messages from Rev. Rose, I became a believer. In the fall of 1947, at the age of ten, I was baptized.

During the summers, I never missed a Vacation Bible School. I attended even before I was officially baptized, as the Bible school was held in our one-room school house. For two weeks we'd learn Bible verses and repeat them in front of the class to get our reward. Each verse was written on a narrow strip of colored paper. With each successful memorization of the passage, we would be able to add it to our Bible chain. By the end of the two weeks, I was proud to have a rainbow array of links to form a pretty necklace. My favorite verse was, and still is, John 3:16

For God so loved the world that he gave his only begotten Son, that whosoever believeth in him should not perish, but have everlasting Life. (King James version)

I find this particular verse to be the bedrock of my faith. At the end of the two week session, there would always be a gathering and a program by the students. In closing, the minister would always ask us to bow our heads and pray. "Raise your hand if you love Jesus and are saved." Momma said that my hand was always the first to fan the air in acceptance and jubilation . I asked Momma how she knew that. Hadn't she closed her eyes in prayer?

Because I had showed so much enthusiasm about God, one day He showed His enthusiasm about me by directing Fern Gauby to save my life. It was the end of Bible School Vacation, and as usual, we had a picnic and a chance to wade in Ash Creek that bordered Grandpa's farm. The creek was shallow, but there were sandbars and hidden sink holes. Splashing around in the cool water was delightful on this June day. We began playing a game called "Crack the Whip". Everyone held hands to form a long line. Then the leader would run as fast as he could and zig-zag through the creek. The object was to break or "crack" the chain. Well, wouldn't you know it -- I was on the tail end. As the rest of the classs rounded the bend of the creek, I lost hold of a classmate's hand and was whipped into a deep area. I couldn't swim and I was in water over my head. I remember seeing the sun rays shining in the murky green water as I came up for air. My arms and legs were flailing as I tried to get to the creek bank. All I was doing was churning the water. I came up a second time, but I couldn't get a footing. Down I went again! As I was coming up for the third time, gasping for breath ; Fern Gauby, an older student helper, grabbed me and pulled me to the bank. I was choking and spitting up green water with particles of sand in it. The teachers and students hovered around me. Fern patted my back and I was able to take deep breaths and come to my senses.

I know that God's hand was in this event. He made the classmate, whose handgrip I had lost, yell out, "Where's Rosemary?" God was there to watch over me and to send Fern to my rescue. I was very thankful, yet I never revealed this episode to my parents. Why? I guess I didn't want to frighten them. Had they heard about it from the other families whose children witnessed the event? I don't know. In looking back, Fren should have been honored for her bravery. In my heart I have regretted that I kept silent about all of this; but in my heart I hold her in loving esteem.

The near-drowning made me more fearful of water. I have never learned to swim, even though I took swimming lessons in a college physical-ed course. I wanted to be able to swim and I thought that a professional instructor and a pool would be the answer to conquering my fear of water. I revealed my story to the teacher, not to gain sympathy, but to let her know just how fragile I was in the water. I did well and I felt that I was making progress. Since it was a "Pass" -"Fail" course, I didn't have to perfect my strokes -- just keep afloat! When finals came around, one routine was to dive off the diving board. I made an excellent entry, cutting the water nice and clean without splashes. I guess I was too proud of myself because my smooth entry was not at all like the "belly flop" that the girl before me had done. My foolish pride weighed me down because I began to sink. I hovered near the bottom and my old fear of drowning came back. Another fear, that of failing the course, came to my mind. The instructor saw my dilemma and immediately got the long bamboo pole and came to my rescue. Did I fail the course? No. I had done all the work that was required and the teacher said that I showed a lot of courage. God was at work in my life again. He knows I can't swim.

Looking back, God had been with me all the time. He saved me and my family during a tornado; He helped me find Jiggs; He healed my appendectomy infection; and He welcomed Grandma into Heaven and sent me a shooting star to prove it. Perhaps the greatest gift of all was the gift of Family. I was truly blessed! I am truly blessed!

My Imaginary Friends

Since my brother and sister were older, they left home when I was about five or six. I missed the raucous times that we'd have together; and when they left for work on their own, I had to find ways to amuse myself. I knew that I couldn't have a girlfriend over to my house everyday; so I created imaginary friends -- ones that would play the way that I wanted them to play.

Every Saturday afternoon, the Major Theater would show a matinee that appealed to the kids, while the parents went about their shopping. I loved the movies with William Boyd as "Hopalong Cassidy". Then too, I enjoyed Esther Williams and Ricardo Montalbon in bullfighting sagas. So, the stage was set for my make-believe theater on the farm. I'd get one of Daddy's wooden sawhorses, the kind used in construction work. I'd find a cowboy hat, toy pistol, and jump on the back of my wooden steed and gallop into the sunset. At other times, I'd be the lady in distress and be saved by an imaginary Hopalong. I'd cling for dear life onto the wooden horse until I reached safety.

One day I asked Daddy if I could play with the pair of long-horns that were mounted on his garage wall. They were only collecting dust out in the workshop. I had big plans for them! Of course Daddy agreed and got them down from the wall. I had managed to find some discarded rope from the building of my tree swing; so with a great deal of lifting and balancing, I managed to get the pair of horns tied to the wooden saw horse.

How proud I was to see that I had created a really fine bull -- just like the one that Esther Williams had in one of her movies. I secretly looked around in the closet to find clothes that either Momma or Dorothy had pushed to the back. I found a black velvet hat, a pair of black pedal-pushers of Dorothy's, and a red paisley print scarf that belonged to Momma. Of course I asked permission to use these items. I had learned to ask after the potholder episode earlier; but I didn't tell Momma how I was planning to use them. She knew that I was busy hatching up some scheme; and that was all right with her. It kept me busy and out of trouble. It was weeks later that she spied me playing bull fighter. Ole!

Then in a more serious mode, I did a re-make of the movie **Spellbound,** that starred Gregory Peck and Ingrid Bergman. For this adventure, I needed a notebook and a pair of black horn-rimmed glasses to play the part of the psychiatrist who was treating Gregory Peck. I donned a pair of Daddy's old reading glasses and played the part of Ingrid Bergman who was analyzing the handsome man. I played that for hours and hours after school. I can't remember if my "Gregory" ever got well -- but I sure spent time with him!

When the wheat harvest was completed and the combine was parked behind the garage, I found that the rotating in-take wheel made a perfect Ferris wheel for my dolls. I'd tie them on with yarn and spin them around and around on the wheel as I pretended to be a carnival worker. When that scenario played out; I'd transform the huge piece of equipment into a river boat. The big wheel was now a paddle-boat in the river taking me upstream to meet characters like Tom Sawyer and Huck Finn.

Of course my dogs were my live companions. In the fall when the corn was cut and stacked in Indian teepee shocks, Rags and I would become Indians. Many a crisp, fall afternoon found us fighting the white man, doing dances around the shocks, or pretending to hunt buffalo. I had a bow and arrow and I found chicken feathers for a head-band; so I tried to dress the part of an Indian. I never went so far as to concoct war paint. I didn't think Momma would have liked the wash-day mess.

For one week I was able to have a Shetland pony when a little boy's family was going on vacation. They asked if we would take care of "Sugar", the sweetest little pony that I had ever known. She was only 36 inches high from her back to the ground. The owner said that his son didn't get along with "Sugar" -- she would nip at him when he tried to feed her carrots or sugar cubes. I didn't have any trouble with her. In fact, I loved the feel of her velvet lips on the palm of my hand as I fed her. I hadn't started school yet, so I was just five years old; but I had a wonderful seven days riding and grooming her. I really wanted to keep her, and the family probably wanted to sell her; but Daddy said that keeping a pony was too expensive in those hard times. I missed "Sugar" when she left and I hoped that the boy would treat her kindly so that she wouldn't nip at him.

Indoor play consisted of playing school at my little green desk in the kitchen corner. My dolls were my students and I held classes in reading and writing (more like my telling stories and scribbling on Big Chief tablet paper). When I became tired of teaching, I'd switch to mothering my dolls.

When I was ten, Roy and Ginny had been married for two years and were expecting their first baby. This was so exciting for me and I insisted on having a doll that drank and wet. Momma thought that I was a little old for that, but she gave in and got one for me. She even knitted me a pair of wool "soaker" pants to cover my doll's diaper -- exactly like the ones that she knitted for the baby. That was the rage in that day because plastic pants were not available to cover the cloth diapers. It was a time before the use of the disposable diapers that now create huge landfills. In that day white cotton diapers were used. They were always so soft and could be used for burp cloths, too. The daily routine was to soak, launder, and fold the diapers.

With my vivid imagination, I traveled to exotic places, rafted down rivers, had various occupations, and met wonderful movie star characters. One dream that was always in the back of my mind was to live in a big city, with lots of people. Momma would tell me , "You can be lonely in a big city as well as on an isolated farm. When my mother, your grandma, died, I was in St. Louis and I was all alone even though there were hundreds of people around."

Of course that observation fell on ten year old deaf ears; but I realized the truth of it when I eventually went to college, married, and settled in big cities. I found that the bigger the city, the more difficult it was to attend major events that I often dreamed of as a child. Usually the ticket price would be prohibitive for a young family and the location and parking status would make the outing seem unbearable -- thus, the enjoyment became somewhat diluted. It was not like the childhood days when my imagintion whisked me away and gave me front row seats!

Perhaps that is why I find being by myself very satisfying. I have never had the urge to travel. When I do travel, I'm always ready to return to my home. Home is my perfect place filled with love and good sensations. I no longer imagine places and things. My wonderlust of childhod has been replaced with satisfaction and contentment. I consider my contentment as my greatest wealth.

Little Lady waiting for "Hopalong

"Work" is the Word

Now I come to the "work" part of my childhood. With the carefree days of youth quickly coming to an end; I was expected to help. It was these chores that helped me appreciate the hard work that a farmer's wife does. At a young age, I was expected to help clean the house. That's the usual duty of a mother and daughter. With Dorothy away from home, I was Momma's right hand gal.

The first duty of spring was to plant a garden. Daddy always prepared the patch with the aid of his plow and harrow. Then it was Momma's and my turn to raise the garden. This seemed like fun in the beginning -- like playing in dirt; however, the soil had to be worked back and forth to eliminate the little clods. It seemed like the dirt would never become smooth and even. "Keep working on the clods, Rosemary. The seeds are tiny and they can't move the clumps of earth." It made me wonder how seeds grew in their natural habitat. I had seen things growing out of the rock crevices along the highways. Why couldn't these Burpee seeds from the package do the same?

Momma insisted that the rows had to be straight and long. I learned to snap a line from one end of the row to the other. There had to be enough space between rows to allow for easy maintenance and harvest. Then we had to know where certain plants could be raised. Carrots, radishes, and lettuce were what Momma called "neat" growers. They stayed in the rows nicely. String beans and peas lopped all over the place; so we didn't plant them near each other in order to prevent inter-tangling. Before we began to dig the rows, Momma put the tiny seeds in a saucer and placed the package picture on the stake at the end of the row. That gave us an idea that the carrots and radishes would be between the peas and string beans. The bright colored pictures gave us promises of things to come if we planted correctly and Mother Nature co-operated.

Digging the trenches for the seeds was the second chore. "Don't dig too deeply. These little seeds will die before they reach the top of the soil." Again, Momma's advice was always to be heeded. Some seeds had to be planted deeper than others, so I had to pay attention. "Don't put the seeds too close together. They need room to grow." Again I thought of how things grew in the wild. How did they do it without Momma's advice?

With the planting accomplished, we had to carefully cover the seeds and tamp down the soil. I was in charge of getting the sprinkling cans lined up by the well, and we carried water to our new garden. With a sprinkling of well water and the bright Kansas sun, the seeds would grow in no time. I kept watch over the rows and was always delighted when the first sprouts appeared. It was my job to tend the rows to keep the weeds at bay. I learned to differentiate between good plants and weeds.

With the succes of our planting, we now had the chores of harvesting and canning the produce. I recall snapping green beans, shelling peas, and slicing carrots in preparation for freezing in the food locker in town. We didn't have a home freezer, so a large unit was rented at the food locker. It flash-froze the vegetables and kept them at peak condition for many months. How good it was to eat those foods in the dead of winter.

My Grandpa was an avid gardener, too. He raised sweet corn, tomatoes, cantaloupes, watermelons, and cherries. Momma canned the tomatoes because they couldn't be successfully frozen; but we froze the corn and cherries. Picking the cherries was a chore that I did not like. The birds would always fly around us as we perched on ladders to get the fruit. We were robbing them of the red, ripe fruit that they found so delicious. If picking cherries wasn't to my liking, then pitting them was even worse. It was so monotonous to "sit and pit" all day. My brother-in-law, John, would tease me about my "sitting and pittting". It did have a funny connotation to it. By the end of cherry season, my hands would be stained brown by the acid in the fruit.

Perhaps the biggest chore was to prepare the chickens for processing in the freezer. Momma always wrung the birds' necks. How she ever learned to do it, I never really knew. You must remember that Momma was raised in the city and she learned this death method when she moved to the farm as a young wife. She had a knack of holding the bird's head in her hand and with one sharp twist of her wrist, the head and body separated into a frenzy of blood-spurting and flopping from the be-headed bird on the ground. At first I couldn't watch the massacre; but Momma was adept at doing it. It was either that procedure or getting out the chopping block and axe. She preferred this simpler method.

While this slaughter was taking place, I was in the kitchen boiling water in order to scald the feathers off the bodies. The feathered body would be dunked into the hot water for a few seconds in order to release the plumage. Then the chicken would be brought up out of the water and the chore of plucking the feathers began. If the water was the right temperature, the feathers would pull off easily. I believe the expression, "You got a good scald on that", came about when something was successful, or good, and easy, like the removal of the soaked feathers. The smell of hot, wet feathers is one I have never forgotten. It's about as bad as a wet dog -- maybe worse. Some farmers saved and cleaned the feathers to make pillows and feather beds; but Momma didn't do that.

When the chickens were plucked, the next step was to cut them into parts and put them in plastic freezer bags. By eleven, I was able to cup up a chicken. I could handle a sharp knife with a great deal of dexterity. I made this chore a little less boring by pretending that I was a noted surgeon. Yes, my imagination was at work again! When I removed the entrails (guts), I had to separate the liver and heart and gizzard. Then I had to cut off the legs, arms (wings), and take out the lungs and kidneys from the back. I hacked away like a Civil War surgeon! I suppose my fantasies in my early childhood got me through the days of chicken cleaning. One day Momma and I prepared 25 young fryers for the freezer. That was quite a day's work. Since I have left the farm, I have never had fresh fried chicken. What a wonderful treat it was!

Momma shared her cooking skills with me. I learned how to prepare meals and desserts. I was with her when the harvest crews came in for lunch. Seems strange to me now that workmen on the farm expected a dinner; but if they worked for someone in town, they went to the local café. Those city wives had it easy; but then there is nothing like good farm cooking with all fresh food. How could the workers resist?

While the farm work was hard, it was also worthwhile. How rewarding to see plants thrive and produce lush crops, to see livestock mature and bring a good price at market; and to see God's hand in nature all around. I can't imagine growing up with concrete streets and sidewalks; with corner stores nearby; and the noise of traffic and neighbors. I loved the solitude of the country -- I still do. I recall the starry nights that could only be enjoyed in the wide open country and to enjoy the Northern Lights. I liked to call them the aurora borealis because it sounded so exotic. The eerie howl of coyotes on a moonlit night could serenade you as you fell asleep and the crowing of the rooster could awaken you in the morning. Cooing of turtle doves as they sing their love song in the twlight hours could soften any heart. Meadow larks that flew from fence post to fence post with a melodic song could make any old grouch smile. How charming to see a covey of quail hurriedly crossing the gravel road to find safety in the field across the way. The lowing of cows in the pasture and the whinnying of horses added to the music of a farm. Some of the birds no longer exist because of climate changes or hunting practices; but they are in my memories of the farm. In my eyes and ears, their existence made the farm a richer place to live.

Putting Away Childish Things

As I began to share more and more of the duties of farm life, I began to learn the responsibilities that come with adulthood. I became capable of doing things alongside my mother; so I found myself putting away the fantasies and imaginary play that filled my early years. At the age of thirteen, I was noticing changes in my body and in my mind. I looked at life in a more pragmatic way. I knew that entering high school would be a dramatic change for me -- no longer in one room with one teacher; but many rooms, many students, and many teachers.

As the hormones began to rage, as they do in all teens, I was becoming interested in romantic things. I wanted my appearance to be spotless, so when bouts of acne occurred, I would be upset. Momma told me that it was all a part of growing up and that others my age were going through the same thing. Of course her: "This too shall pass" quote often irritated me, but I was young and I needed to be reminded of the truth from time to time.

I began to put away my Thomas C. Hinkle books about horses, and picked up Thomas Costain books about history and romance. Today I can't recall the Persian wars that Costain wrote about, but I do recall the steamy love scenes depicted in his novels. I didn't hide this from Momma. In fact, I would read steamy passages to her and we'd laugh and blush together. Our relationship was so pure and honest that we could and did talk about EVERYTHING! This was such a good foundation for my teenage years.

Perhaps I really realized that I was no longer a child when Superintendent Darby addressed the freshman class of Washington High School in 1950. He greeted the 45 freshmen by saying, "Ladies and Gentleman, welcome to Washington High School." He didn't refer to us as "kids" or "guys", but as ladies and gentlemen. What's more, he expected us to act as such. I also found that Mr. Darby, as well as the teachers, addressed us by our sir names. It made me feel mature to be announced as "Miss Dague".

So I close these memoirs at the time when I considered myself a young woman and no longer a child. Oh, there's a spirit in me that will always be "childish", but the events that occurred to me in my youth have made me the person that I am today. This adage is true: "You can take the girl out of the country; but you can't take the country out of the girl." Even now, after living 55years in cities, I still have gravel in my shoes!

Down the Dusty Road – Where are They Now?

Rosemary Dague Coplin Dahlberg

After graduating from Washington High School, Washington, Kansas in 1954, I entered Kansas State College in Manhattan, Kansas and graduated in 1958 with a BS in English/Education. I began my English teaching career at Washington High School in Bethel, Kansas --a suburb of Kansas City, Kansas. It was there that I met my first husband, Bill Coplin.

I stepped aside from my teaching career to tend to my three children. Mark, Steven, and Suzanne. The deaths of Steven at the age of 15 months and Suzanne at the age of 32 years, left deep holes in our hearts. Bill died in 2002, the same year that Suzanne passed.

Overcoming grief, I became a pre-school teacher in an early childhood center. It was a task that I dearly loved. Working with children made me feel alive after the traumatic loses.

After five years of widowhood, I rekindled a freindship with a friend and colleague of my late husband. We married in 2006 and reside in a beautiful retirement community in Rolla, Missouri. Since leaving the farm in 1954, I have returned only to visit.

Mark and Norma Coplin; and sons, Bryan, Steven, and Keith
My son and his family reside in the home that Bill and I owned in St. Louis County, Missouri. Mark is remodeling the house and making it his own. I trust that he has fond memories of his childhood there.

"Daddy and Momma"
Carl Howard Dague died August 29, 1985
Clara Elizabeth Meyrose Davenport Dague died February 16, 1992

"Grandpa and Grandma"
George Henry Lincoln Dague died November 21, 1961
Mary Hyland Dague died September 9, 1947

"My Brother and his Wife"
Roy Corlieu Davenport died September 29, 2003
Virginia Ann Quinn Davenport died September 24, 2005

"My Sister and her Husband"
Dorothy Virginia Davenport Dye (She resides in her home in Wichita, Kansas.)
John Douglas Dye died November 15, 1971

Poop-Poop-a-Doop" Beatrice Hawkenson -- deceased
Mr. Wayne Wilgers and all friends and neighbors --no data, just fond memories!

Printed in the United States
By Bookmasters